TWICE TOLD TALES
A Masonic Reader

TWICE
TOLD TALES

A Masonic Reader

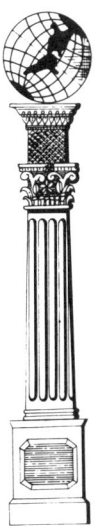
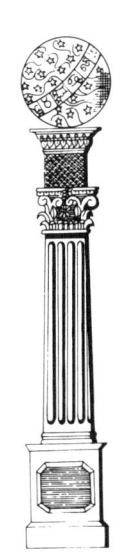

L.C. Helms

Macoy Publishing & Masonic Supply Co., Inc.
Richmond, Virginia

Copyright, 1985

Macoy Publishing & Masonic Supply Co., Inc.
Richmond, Virginia

ISBN-0-88053-081-2

Library of Congress Catalog Card Number 85-61083

Printed in the United States of America

Author's Preface

Masonic history is filled with interesting vignettes that are often tucked neatly away in the folds of larger stories, or sometimes relegated to brief mention in larger comprehensive encyclopedias. This small book is intended to show the human side of Masonic history, a history that is often told and retold only as related to symbols, esoteric discourses on ritual and glowing descriptions of famous Masonic personalities.

Most of the stories in this book relate to people or events that are only footnotes in the larger stream of Masonic history, but footnotes often clarify the larger stories and make them easier to understand. In any event, these are stories the author found interesting and would like to pass along to the reader. I hope you enjoy them as well.

March, 1985   L. C. HELMS

Acknowledgments

My heartfelt thanks to Harry Sharpe of Yakima, Washington and Rose Gilkison of Medford, Oregon for giving me constant access to the Scottish Rite libraries in their cities.

Also, to Vern LaBay of Ellensburg, Washington for his advice and guidance; and, finally, to General Albert Pike who showed me it was quite acceptable to be a compiler as well as a primary researcher.

Contents

Illustrations

REVELATIONS COMPLÈTES
SUR LA FRANC-MAÇONNERIE

LÉO TAXIL

LES FRÈRES
TROIS-POINTS

NOUVELLE ÉDITION

PREMIER VOLUME

PARIS
LETOUZEY ET ANÉ, ÉDITEURS
17, RUE DU VIEUX-COLOMBIER, 17

I
Leo Taxil: A Twice-twisted Tale

"Almost every man wastes part of his life in attempts to display qualities which he does not possess, and to gain applause which he cannot keep."

Samuel Johnson
The Rambler, 1850

"**O** f all the hoaxes perpetrated in the world's history, none surely is more amazing than the one concerning Leo Taxil..." Thus writes Albert G. Mackey when discussing a Jesuit educated adventurer of the late nineteenth century who first appeared to write of damning anti-religious Freemasonic rituals, but who later proved to be a profound embarrassment to the Roman Catholic Church and the anti-Masonic movement.

Leo Taxil was the pen name of Gabriel Antoine Jogand-Pages, a roguish freethinker who lived in Paris during the last quarter of the nineteenth century. *Freethinker* was a term applied to individuals of that era who rejected authority and dogma, especially in religious thinking, in favor of rational inquiry and speculation. W.G. Sibley, in *The Story of Freemasonry*, a 1913 book published only six years after Taxil's death, describes him as being "talented, audacious, and holding both religion and decency in contempt..." Mackey is equally unflattering in his description: "[Taxil was]...careless about the truth, gifted with a lively imagination and an outstanding audacity..."

But, who was Leo Taxil and what relation did he have to Freemasonry and to the anti-Masonic movement?

Leo Taxil first appeared on the international scene in Paris and was immediately known for his acid anti-Catholic publications. This is not unusual given his affiliation with the so-called freethinker groups of that period. He first authored a work entitled *The Private Loves of Pope Pius IX*, and then established an anti-Catholic journal, the *Anti-Clerical*. He was one of several freethinkers who gained a reputation for being a dangerous enemy of the Catholic Church. He was roundly denounced by the Church and excommunicated.

Just as Taxil's early life is unknown and somewhat of a mystery, why he decided to petition the Masonic Order for admission is unclear; especially in view of his freethinking rejection of organized authority and dogma. It may be hypothesized that his personal anti-Catholic feelings led him to believe he would find allies in Masonic lodges. Perhaps his plan for later Masonic exposés was already developed. No one will ever know for sure, but in 1881 he petitioned the French Lodge, *Le Temple de L'Honneur*, to receive the Masonic degrees.

It is reported that there was some hesitancy among the members of the Lodge toward accepting Taxil's petition. Objections were raised concerning his conflicts with the civil authorities as well as with the grossness of his anti-Catholic publications. His espoused views on freethinking also presented doubts as to the seriousness of his desire to affiliate with the Craft. Nonetheless, after assurances from his sponsors, the objections were set aside and Taxil was allowed to take the First Degree. That is as far as Taxil progressed, however, and after being accused of some undisclosed Masonic transgression, he was expelled from the Fraternity and prohibited from taking additional degrees. Unfortunately, as Freemasons were to learn, the damage had been done. As Neitzsche so aptly stated, "No one lies as much as the indignant do."

Again, conjecture must suffice because Taxil's next actions are extremely curious unless one subscribes to the theory that his plans were drawn and completed long before he first petitioned the Parisian lodge. In any event, after being expelled from the Masonic Order, Taxil immediately sought rapprochement with the Catholic Church. Surprisingly, after spending a few months in a monastery and after a public confession of past sins, Taxil was accepted back into the Church. He immediately commenced a vicious and unchecked attack against Freemasonry with the same vigor and energy he had previously reserved for attacking the Catholic Church. Taxil simply switched sides and targets, former ally became enemy and enemy became friend. The fact that he was able to carry out such a transition lends credence to Oscar Wilde's contention that "Perhaps one never seems so much at one's ease as when one has to play a part." How great a role Taxil played was yet to be discovered.

From 1885 to 1886, Taxil published a series of anti-Masonic exposés under the general title of *The Complete Revelations upon Freemasonry*. The series was very popular and Taxil enjoyed new fiscal prosperity and became a minor celebrity. It is at this point, the tale takes yet another strange twist. Taxil's wife, Madame Jogand, continued to publish and sell his earlier anti-Catholic Church books while Taxil was using his newfound political base with the Church to publish and sell his anti-Masonic publications. With the luxury afforded by historical hindsight, it is plain to see that the couple was exploiting the fears, hatred, and myopic visions of all factions involved. Taxil cleverly played his role and profited from being all things to all people: he was pro-Catholic, anti-Catholic, pro-Mason and anti-Mason, depending on the time frame being studied.

Taxil's anti-Masonic writings were the product of a fertile imagination, encouraged by the Church and fueled with financial successes. His anti-Masonic themes were filled with devil worship, murder, torture, and other luridly described obscene behavior. Translated into German and other foreign languages, Taxil became immensely popular and came to the favorable attention of the Catholic Church's ruling hierarchy in Rome. Taxil wrote fictitiously of his own initiation where he said he was led blindfolded into a darkened room, forced to kneel and to stab a shorn sheep to death under the impression that he was executing a renegade Freemason marked for death by the Fraternity. Although he admitted his own initiation was a sham, other men, he alleged, did indeed have to murder members of the Masonic Order who had deviated from Masonic laws and were earmarked for execution. Incredulously, his wildly imaginative and purely fictitious ramblings were accepted by a gullible public.

Taxil's anti-Masonic tales gained him high visibility, financial success, and a great deal of personal popularity. What prompted him to elaborate on his already popular themes must be left to the academic hypotheses of psychologists and psychiatrists. Nonetheless, in 1895, ten years after his first exposés were published, Taxil began producing letters from a woman named Diana Vaughn who claimed to have firsthand knowledge of satanic cult practices occurring within Masonic lodges in the United States. Her knowledge, Taxil asserted, was gained through her father, who started such a cult in a lodge in Louisville, Kentucky, and through her own initiation into a Masonic body. As shocking as Miss Vaughn's revelations were; ripples of shock and indignation over the matter were amplified when she informed the world that her initiation was conducted by no less a Masonic personage than General Albert Pike. Curiously, no one ever spoke to Diana Vaughn or had personal contact with her other than Leo Taxil, but he explained this situation by announcing an imminent death threat on Vaughn's life if the Masons knew where she was hiding. Taxil's explanation appeared to satisfy most skeptics and his anti-Masonic activities continued unchecked.

While the Roman Catholic Church's Cardinal Parocchi thought he was exchanging letters with Diana Vaughn, through Leo Taxil, Taxil and his wife continued their publishing and sale of pro- as well as anti-Masonic literature. Taxil helped orchestrate a large anti-Masonic congress held in 1896 and actually constituted an anti-Masonic central committee. Leo Taxil had risen to new heights of popularity and power in the anti-Masonic movement and his previous transgressions against the Catholic Church seemed ancient history. He was feted for his ardent service to the Church in revealing the true devil worshiping nature of Freemasonry. On occasion a voice was raised asking for proof or clarification, but Taxil's response was similar to the following dialogue, when a German priest asked for details of Diana Vaughn's conversion to Catholicism and subsequent activities. Taxil responded:

> What you are doing [by asking such questions] turns to the benefit of the Freemasons. I swear to have seen Miss Diana with my own eyes, but am not able to indicate the convent that shields her.

Such explanations appeared satisfactory.

Baltasar Gracian, writing in *The Art of Worldly Wisdom*, almost 250 years before Taxil's anti-Masonic exposés, penned the following observation: "One deceit needs many others, and so the whole house is built in the air and must soon come to the ground." On April 17, 1897, the fabric of deceit so cleverly woven by Leo Taxil came apart. As with other major twists in this tale why it occurred only Taxil knows, for it was of his own volition, not through outside force or independent investigation, that the truth finally came to the surface.

On that day in April, Taxil addressed a sizable crowd gathered in the large Geographic Society Hall in Paris, presumably to hear yet another anti-Masonic diatribe. Without warning or foreshadowing of any type, Taxil admitted that the previous twelve years of anti-Masonic writings and stories were complete fabrications and a gigantic hoax. He blithely stated:

> My Reverend Fathers, I sincerely thank my colleagues, the Roman Catholic Press, and our Lords, the Bishops, of having so excellently assisted me to construct a work, the finest and greatest of all my trickeries.

And what of Diana Vaughn? He further stated that Miss Vaughn was a figment of his imagination, and the only woman he ever knew by that name was a secretary some two decades past.

The anti-Masonic crowd, divested of umbrellas and other potential offensive weapons upon their entrance into the hall that night, after hearing Taxil's admission and realizing their own dupery, grew angry, and Taxil was forced to beat a hasty retreat through a prearranged back-door escape.

Shocked incredulity gave way to extreme anger. One Church official damned Taxil to hell, but in deference to the other denizens of that locale, allowed how other condemned souls would turn away from Taxil in embarrassment. Fearing for his safety, or perhaps because his now favorable financial position, Taxil and his wife immediately disappeared from public view. Taxil was well aware of his own viability from that point forward and of Shakespeare's observation that "Men shut their doors against a setting sun."

Aftermath

In retrospect, Taxil proved to be an embarrassment to all parties concerned. His fatuous duplicity harmed the Freemasons, but also the anti-Masonic elements that so eagerly swallowed his vivid fictions. Much like a screaming headline that chronicles a lurid murder that later proves to be incorrect, Taxil's unfounded accusations generated considerable anti-Masonic sentiments. The fact that he later recanted and admitted his hoax never erased the stain of the original fabrications. Following the old bromide concerning "where there is smoke there must be fire," to this day some individuals, ignorant of the facts, tell and retell Taxil's stories as the truth. Even after he admitted his hoax, some individuals *wanted* to believe they were true stories. Conversely, those responsible elements in the Catholic Church were profoundly embarrassed by Taxil's admissions, for they sought only the truth, and their own unwitting assistance aided his trickery immensely.

Taxil managed to embarrass all parties concerned, and he effectively contradicted Plautus's belief that "To blow and swallow at the same time is not easy." Taxil's admission revealed the gullibility of the public to seize upon the sensational, and much of the outcry against him was really spawned from self-embarrassment. La Rouchefoucauld spoke to this type of angry reaction:

> What renders us so bitter against those who trick us is that
> they believe themselves to be more clever than we are.

Taxil's sophistry and audacious trickery has earned a prominent place for him in the annals of the world's greatest hoaxes. There are those who undoubtedly applaud Taxil's duplicity and affirm that the forces and counterforces involved got only what they deserved. But, more than the actual deeds or events, one underlying lesson to be learned from this hoax focuses on the essential element of that seemingly nebulous concept known as "truth." Both parties in this hoax were so anxious to find an ally for their respective positions that they were willing to accept the outlandish as fact and the improbable as possible, rather than take the harder, but more satisfying, route to find the truth. Damning those who held a view dissimilar to their own became an end in itself. Deception, hypocrisy, and fraud became acceptable bedfellows.

In the end, no one emerged victorious; although self-styled freethinkers of that era and today must feel their repudiation of authority and dogma is well justified after witnessing the results of Taxil's deception. In reality, Taxil only proved how elusive the search for truth is, and this strengthens Byron's philosophy, as expressed through *Don Juan*:

> Truth's foundation may be clear
> her streams are muddy,
> And cut through such canals of
> contradiction,
> That she must often navigate
> o'er fiction.

NOVENA CONTESTACIÓN

A

"EL CATÓLICO"

CON MOTIVO DE SUS ESCRITOS

DEFENDIENDO LA OBRA DE

LEO TAXIL:

"LOS MISTERIOS DE LA FRANC-MASONERIA".

SUMARIO :— Las opiniones de Voltaire sobre Satanás—Observa
ción—Opinión favorable de la prensa.

SAN SALVADOR.

Imprenta Nacional, Calle de la Aurora, 9.

SEGUNDA CONTESTACION

A "EL CATÓLICO"

CON MOTIVO DE SUS ESCRITOS

DEFENDIENDO LA OBRA DE

Leo Taxil:

"Los Misterios de la Franc-masonería."

———————

———————

SAN SALVADOR.
———
Imprenta Nacional—Calle La Aurora, 9,.

MASONRY

EXPOSED AND EXPLAINED

—BY—

LEO TAXIL

(GABRIEL JOGAND-PAGES)

Former Member of Lodge Les Amis De L'Honneur Français of the Grand Orient of France.

TRANSLATED FROM THE FRENCH.

PRICE, 30 CENTS

ST. LOUIS, MO.:
CHURCH PROGRESS
1891.

LÉO TAXIL et PAUL VERDUN

Les
Assassinats
maçonniques

PARIS

NOUVELLE LIBRAIRIE PARISIENNE

ALBERT SAVINE, ÉDITEUR

12, RUE DES PYRAMIDES, 12

—

Tous droits réservés.

Vollständige Enthüllungen über die Freimaurerei
von Leo Taxil.

Die

Drei-Punkte-Brüder.

Ausbreitung und Verzweigung,
Organisation und Verfassung, Ritual, geheime
Zeichen und Thätigkeit der Freimaurerei.

Autorisirte Uebersetzung aus dem Französischen.

Erster Band.

Freiburg (Schweiz).

Buchdruckerei des Werkes vom heiligen Paulus.

1886

II
The Puzzle of Ahiman Rezon

I s there a Loch Ness monster? Does a Sasquatch or Big Foot really roam the forested Northwest? What happened to Amelia Earhart, Judge Crater, or Jimmy Hoffa? History is replete with such mysteries and puzzles that will probably never be answered; events that cannot be rationally explained or dealt with in a satisfactory manner. Freemasonry has its share of unexplained mysteries, but perhaps none is more perplexing than the title of Laurence Dermott's work, *Ahiman Rezon*.

Laurence Dermott is an interesting Masonic personage. A former Grand Secretary of the Ancient Grand Lodge of England (1752-1771), he dedicated his later life to the advancement of the Ancient Grand Lodge. He was an extremely active Mason serving as the Master of his Blue Lodge as well as occupying other lodge positions. Despite his eventual commitment to the Ancient Grand Lodge, he was, for fourteen years, a leader in the newly organized and competitive Modern Grand Lodge. Dermott's relationship with the Modern Grand Lodge reportedly ruptured when he was accused of forging the Grand Master's name to a warrant of some significance. He then angerly switched allegiance to the Ancient Grand Lodge and became a dedicated critic of the Moderns. An interesting side bar to Dermott's Masonic life focuses on his relationship, or rather the lack of same, with a contemporary Masonic author, William Preston. William Preston, a prolific writer, was an ardent supporter of the Modern Grand Lodge as Dermott was of the Ancients. Although they lived in the same time period, and most certainly would have interacted with one another, neither referred to the other in any of their numerous publications!

Irrespective of Dermott's personal Masonic activities, his name will forever be remembered in lodges of research because of *Ahiman Rezon*. This work is to be remembered,

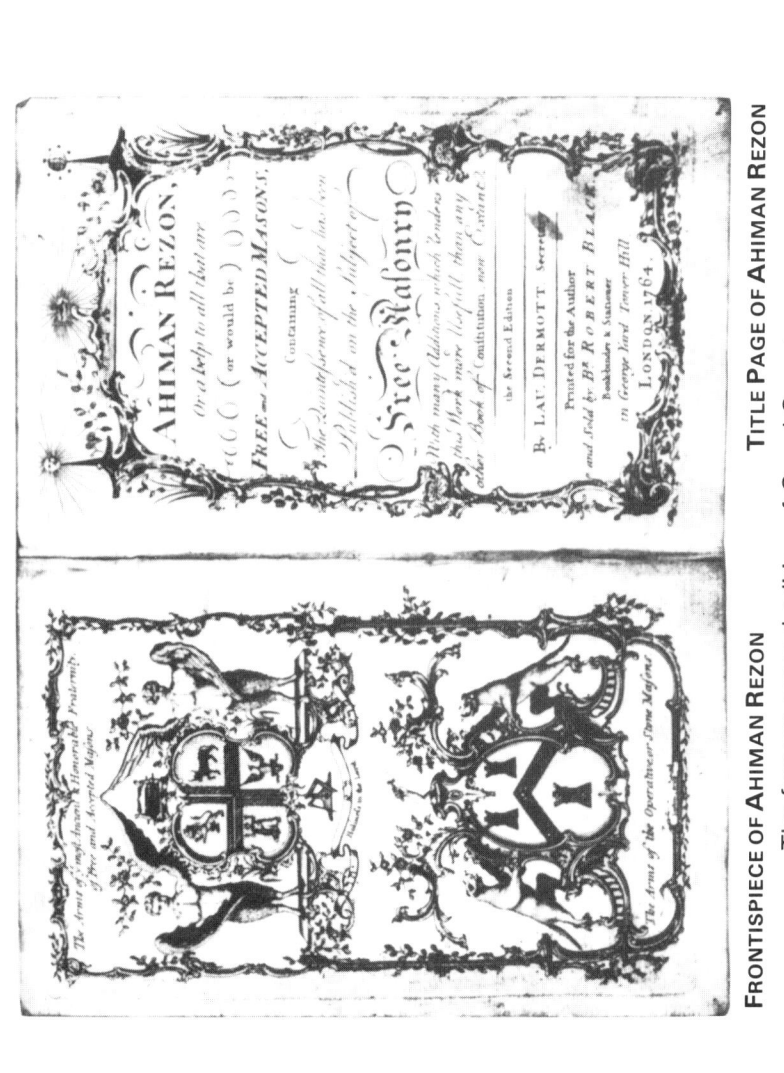

Frontispiece of Ahiman Rezon

Title Page of Ahiman Rezon

The famous second edition of Grand Secretary
Dermott's Monitor and Book of Constitutions.

in part, not for its originality or contribution to new understandings of Masonic history, but simply because of the ambiguity and meaning of the title itself. Henry Coil, in his *Masonic Encyclopedia*, sets the stage for this dilemma:

> Laurence Dermott could have done nothing better to perpetuate his Book of Constitutions for the Ancient Grand Lodge of England than to name it *Ahiman Rezon*, for scholars have been arguing about the meaning thereof for two centuries and some American Grand Lodges apply the term to their Constitutions to this day.

The fact is indisputable that the meaning of the term *Ahiman Rezon* is unclear and probably lost forever. There are several alleged meanings, many in popular use by various respected Masonic bodies today, but none can be more than educated guesses or perhaps even fanciful wishes. What does *Ahiman Rezon* purport to mean?

Dr. Albert Mackey, who it is reported attempted to trace almost every item of Masonic importance to the Hebrew language, claimed the term translated as the "Will of Selected Brethren." In 1919, however, the Pennsylvania edition of *Ahiman Rezon* stated that Hebrew scholars had examined the term and categorically rejected Mackey's definition. Instead, the Pennsylvania publication asserted the term came from the Spanish language. By breaking it into Spanish sounding syllables it hypothesized the term translated as, "Here is the full account of the law." This would be a logical title for a book of rules and regulations, but one might argue that such a phonetic interpretation strains credulity.

Other popular interpretations range from Frederick Dalcho's "Secrets of a Prepared Brother," to W.S. Rockwell's "Royal Builder." Unfortunately, none of the aforementioned attempts at defining the term can be proven correct although each has it proponents. Perhaps the futility of seeking an esoteric answer is best summed up by W.S. Rockwell himself, in the foreword to Daniel Sickel's 1875 book, *The General Ahiman Rezon and Freemason's Guide*. Rockwell, a former Sovereign Grand Inspector General of the Southern Supreme Council and Grand Master of Georgia (1856-1862), examines Dalcho's definition and determines there are several difficulties "which seem to render [Dalcho's] definition inadmissible." He bases his argument, in part, on the inability to achieve the parallel construction needed between English and Hebrew to derive Dalcho's translation. Rockwell then examines Mackey's definition and concludes: "It is true that this definition more nearly accords with what the book contains, than proposed by Dalcho; yet, there would seem to be no less formidable objections to this view..." Again, Rockwell goes to the Hebrew language and by dissecting the syntax and verb structure he proves, to his satisfaction, that Mackey also was incorrect in his assumptions. Unfortunately, Rockwell goes no further. After developing and supporting his linguistic arguments that contradicts both of the major theories, he simply drops the subject and Sickel's book continues with the preface. Rockwell later developed an alternative theory that centered on a translation focusing on "Brother Secretary." This translation may indeed prove more accurate than the others as subsequent events are recalled.

The answer, if there is one, may not lie in some scholarly interpretation of a foreign tongue or an esoteric interpretation of a term vested with hidden meanings. The answer might be discovered in a rather mundane fashion. *Ahiman Rezon* is not an original work of Laurence Demott's. He copied entire sections directly from Edward Spratt's *Irish Book of Constitutions* (1751) which, in turn, was a reiteration of James Anderson's now famous *Constitutions* of 1738. It has been stated that *Ahiman Rezon* does not testify to Dermott's skill as an author. Coil states:

> ...[Dermott's] best contribution to Masonic literature, viz., his *Ahiman Rezon*, fairly fixes the limit of his ability and, regrettably, none too high. It left much to be desired in originality and etiquette...

Dermott, it appears, was none too original in his thoughts and prone to borrow from previously published works.

In the Geneva Bible of 1560, the word *Ahiman* is defined as meaning "a prepared brother of the right hand." *Rezon* is defined as meaning "a secretary." Since Dermott quotes extensively from this edition of the Bible it is quite likely he simply appropriated the terms, combined them, and developed a title for his own book. Combining the two phrases would produce a title that could mean a cypher, monitor or aid to a Brother Freemason, much like a lodge secretary would help or aid a lodge member. Thus, Rockwell's interpretation of "Brother Secretary" appears to have considerable merit. It is hardly a glamorous explanation, but perhaps the most defendable hypothesis.

The fact that Dermott appears to have copied, or even plagerized, other works in the preparation and publication of *Ahiman Rezon* should not cause any great discomfort to those who view his work as a major contribution to Masonic literature. Indeed, in the preface of Albert Pike's *Morals and Dogma* it is stated:

> In preparing this work, the Grand Commander [Pike] has been about equally Author and Compiler; since he has extracted quite half its contents from the works of the best writers and most philosophic or eloquent thinkers.

Although the material in *Ahiman Rezon* was not new and the title itself is confusing and perplexing, the work had a profound effect. The far reaching ramifications of the work is accurately recorded in the *History of the Ancient and Honorable Fraternity of Free and Accepted Masons*, published in 1923, Henry L. Stillson, editor-in-chief:

> It may be of interest to state that the Regulations published by the Ancient Grand Lodge...known as Ahiman Rezon, were eight in number.

> As the Book of Constitutions became the model or standard for the government of Freemasonry by the Moderns, so the *Ahiman Rezon* was the law of the Ancients.

Whatever *Ahiman Rezon* really means lies buried with Laurence Dermott. It is unimportant, however, when compared to the impact of the book. Whatever disagreements Masons might have over the meaning should be placed in the context described by Saint-Exupery in *The Wisdom of the Sands*. "What sets men at variance is but the treachery of language, for always they desire the same things."

III
Symbolic Enigmas In American Freemasonry

All Freemasons who remain reasonably attentive during their initiations and maintain even semi-regular attendance at lodge realize the Fraternity is pregnant with symbols. Allen Roberts flatly states that "...symbolism is the lifeblood of the Craft," and Alphonse Cerza affirms, "Everything connected with the ceremonies of Freemasonry have a symbolic meaning." Of all the symbols available to catch the public's eye, without a doubt, the most universally recognized symbol of American Freemasonry is the juxtaposition of the Square interlaced with the Compasses.

If queried, most American Freemasons would probably assert that the interlacing of the Square and Compasses is an extremely old, if not ancient, tradition. In reality, the interlacing of the Instruments was introduced rather recently into Masonic history. The use, and misuse, of this Masonic symbol makes interesting history and fascinating reading.

Henry Coil, in his *Masonic Encyclopedia*, focuses on the timeframe when the symbol that is so easily recognizable today first came into existence.

> In early 18th century charts, either the Square or the Compass is often shown without the other and, when they are both included, they are never joined or interlaced or even near each other in the charts until about 1750.

Coil is joined in his evaluation by other Masonic historians such as Roberts and Dr. Albert Mackey. Coil further recalls that even though the Square and Compasses were not depicted in the interlaced form until shortly after the date cited above, soon they began appearing on badges, buttons, and watch fobs.

American Freemasons are accustomed to seeing jewelry and other representations with the letter "G" nes-

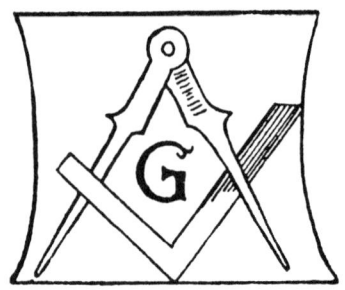

PRINTED IN *PTOLEMY'S GEOGRAPHY* OF 1525.

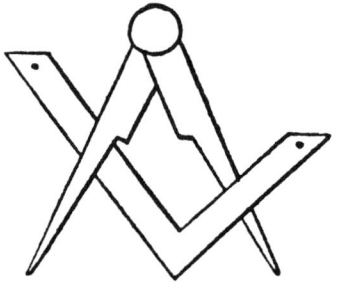

A CARVED SYMBOL OF 1597.

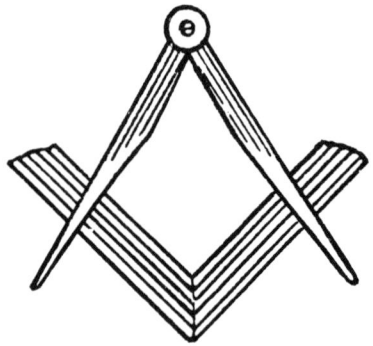

A MODERN SYMBOL USED WITH OR WITHOUT A G IN THE CENTER.

tled between the Square and Compasses; with an explanation usually referenced to "Geometry" or to the first letter of the English-speaking world's Deity. The "G," however, is an even more recent addition to the interlacing, and researchers cannot trace any use of that letter with the Square and Compasses before 1850. There is no disputing the fact that the letter "G" appears in early Masonic catechisms, as it is mentioned in Samuel Prichard's supposed exposé in 1730, and in other rituals, but never in juxtaposition with the Square and Compasses. Allen E. Roberts, in *The Craft and Its Symbols*, delved into this subject. When writing about the attempted use of the Square and Compasses by a flour manufacturer in 1873, he wrote:

> It was about this time that some unknown "inventor" added a letter "G" in the center of the Square and Compasses. To many American Masons the emblem is not complete without this letter, this is not so in other countries, however. In other languages God does not start with the letter "G"; neither does Geometry.

Some theorists believe the "G" was added to the Square and Compasses by a jeweler, simply as an ornamental design.

The flour manufacturer referred to by Roberts provides an introduction to a series of interesting vignettes that speak to the use of the interlaced Square and Compasses for non-Masonic purposes.

In 1873, the flour manufacturer made application to the United States Patent Office for permission to use the Square and Compasses, as used by American Freemasons, as a trademark. The Commissioner of Patents refused permission using the following rationale:

> If this emblem were something other than precisely what it is — either less known, less significant, or fully and universally understood — all this might readily be admitted. But, considering its peculiar character and relation to the public, an anomalous question is presented. There can be no doubt that this device, so commonly worn and employed by Masons, has established mystic significance, universally recognized as existing; whether comprehended by all or not is not material to this issue.

The commissioner summed up the government's position:

> It will be universally understood, or misunderstood, as having a Masonic significance, and, therefore, as a trademark, must constantly work deception.

Whereas the flour company was prevented from using the Square and Compasses, Harold V.B. Voorhis, in *Facts For Freemasons*, reveals, that others were more successful. In answer to the question, "What are some of the odd uses of Masonic emblems?" Voorhis reports:

> A cattle brand (Square and Compasses) used by Poindexter and Orr Livestock Company, Dillon, Montana, since 1853. Hiram Gasoline Barge, near Highlands, N.J., had a square and compasses on its flag. John Wanamaker had square and compasses in the store entrance floor of the large department store in New York City.

While attending an antique show in San Francisco, I also found an "appropriated" use of the Square and Compasses. An avid collector of Masonic memorabilia, I came across what appeared to be an old stampholder with Masonic symbols on the cover. Once cleaned, however, and examined under a magnifying glass, the emblem proved to be an interlaced square and compasses with an arm and hammer in the middle. After several letters brought no positive results, I was able to track down the answer by contacting Jerry Marsengill of the Philalethes Society. What I had stumbled on was the trademark of the Junior Order of United American Mechanics. This is strange since the flour manufacturer had been denied a copyright on their use of the interlaced square and compasses.

The Square and Compasses, interlaced with the letter "G" in the middle, is undoubtably the most readily identified symbol of American Freemasonry. There is even a fraternity named the "Square and Compass Fraternity" that admits collegiate Freemasons. The name of this fraternity reveals yet another dimension of the continuing saga involving this Masonic symbol. Mackey's *Masonic Encyclopedia* states that the Fraternity's use of "compass" is an embarrassing, but a common, error. A compass, Mackey states, is an instrument for finding direction and has never been used as a Masonic symbol. The instrument depicted on Masonic jewelry, books, and in ritual is used for drawing circles and is properly called "compasses." Coil, however, assumes a different posture. He asserts that compasses is a singular noun in plural form, like scissors, pliers, pants, or trousers. They are mechanically united, but gramatically separate. He refers to *Webster's Dictionary* for a definition of compass. Webster shows one definition as "an instrument for describing circles," and then describes their physical properties: "two pointed branches or legs joined at the top by a pivot."

The confusion as to whether the Masonic symbol is properly a "compass" or "compasses" is further compounded if one examines the aforementioned 1730 exposé, *Masonry Dissected*. In this book, Prichard at one point states: "The Compass extended to my naked Left Breast," but he later recalls, "The Yellow Jacket is the compass." In 1740, another Masonic-related publication refers to a "pair of compasses."

Which is correct? Perhaps correctness in this case is a moot point. Both terms have been used interchangeably since the early eighteenth century. An examination of the 1980 *American Heritage Dictionary of the English Language* reveals support for Coil's position. Both definitions fall under the word compass, but under the definition of an instrument for drawing circles there is a parenthetical note: "sometimes plural." Language, as word meanings, change with custom and useage.

The "Yellow Jacket" referred to by Prichard provides yet another interesting sidebar. In the eighteenth century, and earlier, the compass was often made of brass with blue steel points. Thus, they were labeled "Blue Breeches and Yellow Jackets." It is recorded that some lodges in Scotland interpreted that symbolism so strictly that the Master of the lodge, and sometimes the members, was required to dress in a yellow coat and blue breeches.

Lest the Compass appear to be the focal point of all confusion, the use of the Square has also caused some concern. American Freemasons use a square that has equal length in tne legs. Mackey points out the problem with this representation:

> French Freemasons have almost universally given it one leg longer than the other, thus making it a carpenter's square. American Freemasons... have, while generally preserving the equality of length in the legs, unnecessarily marked its surface with inches; thus making it an instrument for measuring length and breadth, which it is not!

Mackey continues this line of reasoning by pointing out the differences in squares. The Masonic Square is the square of stone masons, the "trying" square with a plain surface intended to test the accuracy of the sides of the stone.

In essence, the error depicting the wrong square on Masonic items and the confusion surrounding the use of the compass makes interesting reading, but this does not affect any basic Masonic tenets. Indeed, the original use of traditional symbols has considerable merit. As Thomas Carlyle stated:

> The merit of originality is not novelty; it is sincerity. The believing man is the original man; whatsoever he believes, he believes for himself, not for others.

IV
Was Jack The Ripper a Freemason?

Was Jack the Ripper a Freemason, or were the series of Ripper-like murders in London's East End in the 1880's planned by Freemasons as a means to keep Prince Eddy and a Masonic dominated government in control of England? As incredulous as those questions might first appear to contemporary Freemasons, that is exactly what is asserted in a book entitled, *Jack the Ripper: The Final Solution* by Stephen Knight. The entire thesis of his book is brought to focus in a chapter entitled, "The Masonic Killers" in which Knight examines each Ripper-like murder and the series of events that led him to conclude that not only did English Freemasons mastermind the murders, but they did so to ensure the continuance of a government heavily dominated by members of the Fraternity.

As incredulous as these statements are to the informed students of Freemasonry, Knight weaves a clever trap. The unsuspecting reader, with little or no knowledge of the inherent nature of Freemasonry, is led to believe that Freemasons are a crafty group of men, intent upon some nefarious purpose and willing to commit murder and treason in order ro achieve this unspecified end. Initiated Freemasons can well scoff at Knight's selective editing of Masonic oaths and his myopic scope of historical inquiry, but just when this writer was about to toss the book aside in amused disgust, Knight revealed the following evidence taken from official police reports and autopsies of the victims of Jack the Ripper.

In all of the Jack the Ripper murders the victims had their throats slashed left to right. Knight points out that all victims were dispatched "according to an age-old Masonic ritual." He fails to note, however, that this would be a nattural motion for a right-handed person.

Another victim had triangular flaps of skin removed from each cheek. Knight asserts that the "sacred sign of Masonry is two triangles, which represents the altar top of the Holy Royal Arch."

In the killing of Annie Chapman all metal and coins had been removed from her body, but not stolen: simply placed beside her. This, Knight asserted, is an obvious allusion to the initiation of Masons when they are divested of all metals during the ceremonies to indicate their poor and penniless position.

Knight points out that the murders all occurred around Mitre Square in London, and the mitre is one of the Free-masons' Working Tools.

Stretching still more to make a point, Knight even found a connection between the number of days between the killings: "There was even significance in the thirty-nine days that were allowed to elapse between the murders of Eddowes and that of Kelly. Thirty-nine is a meaningful number to Freemasons, arrived at by multiplying the 'per-fect' number 3, by the favorite number thirteen. In other words it is the ideal, the perfect number of favorites."

On the wall near the body of one victim the following message was scrawled: "The Juwes are The men That Will not be Blamed for nothing." The police erased the message fearing anti-Jewish riots if Londoners felt Jack the Ripper somehow related to Jews. Knight, however, interprets the sign differently. He feels it was a direct allusion to the three Apprentice Masons who killed Hiram Abiff!

To come to the crux of Knight's argument, we must first examine the political climate in England during the last quarter of the 19th century, and the cast of characters in-volved in attempting to solve the Jack the Ripper murders.

Knight believes that Queen Victoria's monarchy was not popular. Civil strife, economic woe and political dis-turbance had given rise to antimonarchial thought, and the sentiments for socialism was growing yearly. Victoria's grandson was Prince Eddy, later the Duke of Clarence. Prince Eddy, Knight asserts, was not the type of man mon-archists would like to have to restore a weakening monarchy. Eddy, as he was known, was reputed to be fond of venturing into the less savory parts of town for affairs with local ladies of the night. Key individuals in the government were afraid that Eddy's involvement with prostitutes and other ladies, married and single, plus his escapades in the divorce courts, might help topple the monarchy.

Jack the Ripper, he asserts, was not one man, but rather a small group of Freemasons intent upon preserving their favored place in government. Sir Charles Warren, the Commissioner of Metropolitan Police, was a high ranking Freemason as was his assistant commissioner, Sir Robert Anderson. The Prime Minister, Salisbury, was a Freemason, as was the Queen's physician, Sir William Gull. Both Prince Eddy and his father, the Duke of Wales, were Freemasons. In fact, most major and minor officials in England at that time had some affiliation with the Fraternity.

Knight theorizes that the series of Jack the Ripper murders were perpetrated by two, perhaps three Freemasons. The police officials used their positions to cover the trail of their Brethren and, indeed, threw false clues to those who tried to discover the truth. Gull, the physician, Knight asserts, probably used his medical training to butcher the women. Warren and Anderson did not attempt to solve the crimes; indeed they served as impediments to justice.

If Freemasons were really intent upon saving the monarchy and keeping themselves in power, they could have certainly found easier, quieter ways to silence five prostitutes than the commission of a series of elaborate, highly bloody murders that caught the attention of every newspaper in England and the imagination of every social revolutionary in London. The scenario, as Knight would have the reader believe, would be similar to two criminals murdering someone, the first criminal leaving his wallet behind so the police could find him, while the second criminal tries to hide the wallet so no one would know who did it. It simply does not make sense. Murder in the London slums was not an unusual event, as Knight himself points out. If five prostitutes with no permanent address and no political connections were to be eliminated, for whatever reason, a series of knifings, stranglings and drownings would have achieved the same end without implicating Freemasonry and, by association, the monarchy. No, Mr. Knight begs the question. He has indeed collected a plethora of facts, but he overlooks the obvious conclusion to be drawn from them.

If you are to discard the idea that there was indeed a crazed maniac who called himself Jack the Ripper (who may have had some knowledge of Freemasonry because the ritualistic murders seemed to parallel certain Masonic oaths too accurately to be incidental), you must ask yourself who would benefit from a series of sensational murders that implicated the government through its association with Freemasons.

Actually, Knight himself provides the answer. If the monarchy and government were indeed in danger of being overthrown and all that was needed was a spark to ignite the discontent, who would profit from that revolution? Obviously the individuals who were attempting to overthrow the government. Knight mentions the socialists, but there were many antimonarchist groups who would have been happy to see Queen Victoria and Prince Edward toppled from the Throne.

It is much more logical to assume that the murders were perpetrated by men intent upon discrediting the government. What better way would there be than to make it appear as if the Freemasons, symbolic of the British Government to many, were actually behind the murders? Once the story of the murders was told, the accompanying story of Eddy would destroy the monarchy. If indeed Knight feels he discovered highly placed Freemasons covering the clues left by the murderers, it was because the investigators knew they were false clues, not left by Freemasons, but left so as to discredit Freemasonry and therefore the government. Knight assumes the police did not pursue the Masonic connection because of secret oaths and obligations to defend one another. He never for a moment pauses to examine the idea that the police were extremely competent and discarded certain "clues" because they knew of their adsurdity from a position within the Craft.

Who was Jack the Ripper? No one knows and undoubtedly no one will ever know. Knight does bring to light new information about the murders that does indeed reveal Masonic implications heretofore previously unpublicized. Unfortunately, Knight moves from fact to conclusion without examining all possible alternatives. The informed reader will close this book not believing the English Freemasons perpetrated the murders, but rather amazed at the abundance of Masonic related clues found at the scene of each murder. Indeed, there are three conclusions to the case, none of which will probably ever be proved.

(1) The Freemasons on the police force came to the conclusion that someone was attempting to cast suspicion on Freemasonry by leaving clues that the murderer or murderers thought followed instructions for Masonic ritualistic murders. Although the culprits were ignorant to the purpose of the Craft's oaths, they knew enough about Masonic ceremonies to leave what they considered to be "evidence" that would indicate Masonic involvement. This involvement they hoped, would incriminate the Freemasons, embarrass the Throne, reveal the weakness of Prince Eddy, and help topple the government.

(2) Jack the Ripper was a deranged maniac who at one time was either a Freemason or knew something of Masonic ritual work. This would explain the so-called Masonic clues left at the scene of each Ripper-like murder.

(3) The ritualistic murders were simply the actions of a maniac and any resemblance between Masonic ritual work and the "clues" are purely happenstance.

Each person will develop his or her own ideas and conclusions as to what actually transpired in London in the 1880's, but it is patently absurd to accept Knight's far-fetched thesis of "The Masonic Killers" being Jack the Ripper.

V
Masonry and Literature

*"The pen is the tongue of the hand—a
silent utterer of words for the ages."*
Henry Ward Beecher (1887)

It should not come as a surprise that a Fraternity that included many of the greatest socio-political activists and philosophers of recent history should also find its name, outward customs and public rituals recorded in the pages of classical and popular literature. Freemasons such as Voltaire, Christopher Wren, Roscoe Pound, Edward Gibbon and Elias Ashmole were easily recognizable and their actions, associations and beliefs influenced societies far beyond the confines of their native lands. These men, plus countless others, exemplified the morals and dogmas of Freemasonry and provided the author, poet and antiquarian of all eras the opportunity to use the Craft as a source of creative inspiration, knowledge and historical reference.

Rudyard Kipling is a prime example of a Freemason who incorporated the Craft's teachings and symbols not only into his personal life, but also in his writing. Kipling often expressed the sentiment that Freemasonry not only confirmed his faith in a common fraternity of mankind, but also reinforced his belief in the desirability of pursuing a common moral code. Of his own Masonic background he was proud of being Initiated into the Craft by a Moslem, Passed by a Hindu and Raised by an Englishman. Kipling's works are punctuated by references to the Craft if the reader is alert to the allusions and descriptions contained therein. Two short stories and poems stand most prominent vis-a-vis Freemasonry. In the tale, *"The Man Who Would Be King,"* Kipling describes two Master Masons who established a kingdom in Kafiristan by using the rituals and ceremonies of Freemasonry in concert with the native popula-

RUDYARD KIPLING

tion's "pagan" rituals. The Masonic tone of this work is established at the onset when one Mason asks the other: "Where have you come from?" and the other answered, "From the East and I am hoping that you will give him the message on the Square." Kipling's second story, *"In the Interest of the Brethren,"* is a more heart-warming tale describing the war-ravaged Brethren who find and frequent a Lodge of Instruction enjoying the rituals and fellowship practiced there. As one Mason so aptly stated, at the Lodge they experienced: "The Fatherhood of God and the Brotherhood of Man; and what more in Hell do you want?"[1]

Kipling's poem, *"Banquet Night,"* prefaces the story, *"In The Interest of The Brethren,"* both of which are found in the larger book *Debits and Credits*. Its direction can be best described by citing one of the verses:[2]

> Carry this message to Hiram Abif
>   Excellent Master of forge and mine:
> I and the Brethren would like it if
>   He and the Brethren will come to dine,
> (Garments from Bozrah or morning dress)
>   As Fellow-Craftsmen — no more and no less.

Kipling's, *"The Mother Lodge,"* is my personal favorite. It illustrates the mingling of men of different colors, creeds and social classes on the common level of the Lodgeroom floor. The following lines still strike a responsive note with contemporary Freemasons:[3]

> Full oft on Guv'ment service
>   This rovin' foot 'ath pressed
> An' bore fraternal greetin's
>   To the Lodges east an' west
> Accordin' as commanded
>   From Kohat to Singapore,
> But I wish that I might see them
>   In my Mother Lodge once more!

and the refrain:

> Outside—Sergeant! Sir! Salute! Salaam!
> Inside—"Brother," an' it doesn't do no 'arm.
> We met upon the Level an' we parted on the Square
> An' I was Junior Deacon in my Mother Lodge out there!

Kipling's autobiography graphically ties Freemasonry to his personal life.[4]

> In '85 I was made a Freemason by dispensation...being under age, because the Lodge hoped for a good secretary. They did not get him, but I applied, and got Father to advise, in decorating the bare walls of the Masonic Hall with hangings after the prescription of Solomon's Temple. Here I met Muslims, Hindus, Sikhs, members of the Arya and Brahmo Samaj, and a Jew Tyler, who was priest and butcher to this little community in the city. So yet another world opened to me which I needed.

Obviously, Rudyard Kipling's Freemasonry was inextricably interwoven with his professional career.

Other noted writers used the subject of Freemasonry as a reference to develop or elaborate a theme. Lew Wallace, for example, the author of *Ben Hur*, developed the scenario first alluding to the antiquity of the Master in another novel, *The Prince of India*, by having the protagonist excavate the hitherto undiscovered tomb of Hiram, King of Tyre. Inside the tomb was found King Solomon's sword and "the instruments sacred then and ever since to Master Masons: a square, a gavel, a plummet, and an inscribing compass."[5] It is interesting to note that the author placed the working tools of a Mason with King Hiram's other treasures; namely, gold, silver and jewels.

Edgar Allan Poe included a passing reference to Freemasonry in a brief passage from *The Cask of Amontillado*.[6]

> I broke and reached him a flagon of De Grave. He emptied it at a breath. His eyes flashed with a fierce light. He laughed and threw the bottle upwards with a gesticulation I did not understand. I looked at him in surprise. He repeated the movement—a grotesque one.
>
> "You do not comprehend?" he said.
>
> "Not I," I replied.
>
> "Then you are not of the brotherhood."
>
> "How?"
>
> "You are not of the Masons."
>
> "Yes, Yes," I said, "yes, yes."
>
> "You? Impossible! A Mason?"

EDGAR ALLAN POE

"A Mason," I replied.

"A sign," he said, "a sign."

"It is this," I answered, producing from beneath the folds of my *Roquelaire* a trowel.

"You jest," he exclaimed.

One can only imagine what type of Masonic sign Poe envisioned that would be both grotesque and identifying. Poe was not the only scribe that described the symbols and rituals of Masonry in quasi-unflattering terms. The immortal Charles Dickens satirized Freemasonry in *Barnaby Rudge* and Mozart's, *"Magic Flute,"* attempts to link Freemasonry in rather uncomplimentary terms to certain ancient Egyptian traditions.

Even Sherlock Holmes was cognizant of Freemasonry. In a light scene that speaks more of Masonry's stature in public consciousness, A. Conan Doyle presented the following scene in *"The Red Headed League."*[7]

> Sherlock Holmes' quick eye...noticed my questioning glances. Beyond the obvious facts that he has sometimes done manual labor, that he takes snuff, that he is a Freemason, that he has been in China...
>
> Mr. Jabez Wilson startled up in his chair, with his forefinger upon the paper, but his eyes upon my companion.
>
> "How, in the name of good fortune, did you know all that, Mr. Holmes?" he asked. "How did you know, for example, that I did manuel labor. It's as true as gospel, for I began as a ship's carpenter."
>
> "Your hands, my dear sir. Your right hand is quite a size larger than your left. You have worked with it, and the muscles are more developed."
>
> "Well, the snuff, then, and the Freemasonry?"
>
> "I won't insult your intelligence by letting you know I read that, especially as, rather against strict rules of your order, you use an arc-and-compass breastpin."
>
> "Ah, of course, I forgot that."

A minor passage to be sure, but indicative of the notoriety Masonry enjoyed during this era. A more presenting example can be found in Count Tolstoi's epic, *War and Peace*. A moral thread of redemption of the novel's main character is woven through the book starting with his Initiation into a Russian Lodge. Robert Burns, himself a Freemason, wrote a stirring ode, *"Farewell to Tarbolton Lodge."* Goethe wrote of Masonic songs, a poem entitled, *"A Mason's Ways,"* and a novel that many believe to be one of the finest Masonic books ever written: *Wilhelm Meister.* Another German, Gottfried Lessing, utilized the Craft in his novel, *Nathan the Wise.* Parallel association can be related to Sir Francis Bacon's *House of Solomon.* The list of Masonic-related literature is obviously enormous and one can only speak of the most salient examples.

The important concept in tracing Freemasonry through literature focuses not on what was written, but rather the fact that the Craft was a focal point of discussion. Freemasonry then, and now, conveyed a message even to the uninitiated and uninformed. Tolstoi used it to show morally desirable behavior as opposed to moral decadence; Kipling saw it as a vehicle for leveling artificial social standards and Wallace used the Craft for conveying quasi-religious messages. Burns wrote of freedom, harmony and the Grand Architect coming to life in and out of the lodge. Others, perhaps, were more mundane in their usage appealing to outward signs and symbols.

In addition to the inclusion of Masonic signs and phrases in general literature, there are countless volumes of Masonic histories, guides, ciphers and books which focus on each author's personal line of expression. Many of these publications lost their objectivity as the authors endeavored to bring forward a particular sentiment. Indeed, even Dr. Anderson's famous *Constitutions* appears somewhat skewed under the scrutinizing eye of history; for example, the language used could easily be interpreted in such a manner that promised more than was forthcoming. As J.M. Roberts stated:[8]

> ...it encouraged both suspicion among the profane and over-optimism about future revelations among the credulous initiated. Such language thus contributed to a general psychosis of secrecy which gripped those who distrusted the craft...Finally, Anderson's language also favoured the

ROBERT BURNS

Installation of Robert Burns as Poet Laureate of Lodge Canongate Kilwinning, March 1, 1787.

elaboration of systems of 'higher degrees' whose existence
was suspected perhaps even before they were devised.

Close on the heels of the publication of Anderson's
Constitutions, came Samuel Prichard's, *Masonry Dissected*, and, of course, a later book entitled, *The Defense
of Masonry*, by Martin Clare. Two decades later Pope Clement XII's Bull of excommunication, *"En Eminenti,"*
caused even more agitation and, eventually, pro and con
Masonic publications. The plethora of literature thus commenced.

In 1772, William Preston published what is generally
regarded as the first Masonic monitor titled, *Illustrations
of Masonry*, in London, England. After Preston, numerous
monitors were published, including several works in
America by such Masons as Chapman, Sickels, Macoy and
Atwood. A Masonic guide published for the Wisconsin
Lodges in 1889, contained the poem, *"The Level and the
Square,"* authored by Rob Morris, that may be the most
widely recognized Masonic poem. A most often repeated
stanza is:

> Hands round, ye faithful craftsmen, in the bright,
>   fraternal chain;
> We part upon the Square below to meet in Heaven
>   again.
> Oh, what words of previous meanings those words
>   Masonic are—
> We meet upon the Level and we part upon the
>   Square.

Of special note is a publication by George Smith in 1783,
entitled, *The Use and Abuse Of Freemasonry*. Prior to this
date only handbooks or monitors sanctioned by a Grand
Lodge had been published. Smith ignored the Grand
Lodge, defied possible sanctions or repercussions, and
published his book. From that date forward, Freemasons
were free to publish craft-related material without prior
censorship.

Since this period literally thousands of books and
pamphlets have been written about Freemasonry. Trivia
buffs will recall that the first use of the term "free mason"

appeared in two books that were published in 1563, one entitled, *The First and Chief Grounds . . . of Architecture*, and the second, *A Book in English Metre, Of The Great Merchant Man Called Dives Pragmatius.*

Finally, no mention of Masonic literature should be made without touching upon a tangent field: musical compositions. In addition to Mozart's *"Magic Flute,"* previously mentioned, other famous composers writing music specifically for or about Freemasonry include Johann Wolfgang Goethe, Robert Burns, Franz Liszt and Jean Sibelius.

The works and authors mentioned thus far represent only a partial list. It is impossible, for a work of this nature, to develop an exhaustive encyclopedia of all related literature.

In summation, what does this compilation of names, works, and dates actually signify to the contemporary Freemason? First, it reveals that Freemasonry was an accepted and acknowledged part of society by the 17th century. Historians place great importance on being able to trace the actual, not the mythological, history of an event, person or organization. Written history, if accurately recorded, in the form of books, poetry, or music, tends to anchor facts, as opposed to oral history which can become more easily distorted, embellished and altered. A great deal of Masonic history can be garnered from a careful examination of the written word.

The use of references to Freemasonry also indicates the position of the Craft in society. A minor inconsequential organization could hardly be expected to generate the type of response and recognition the author hoped to elicit with their allusion to Masonic symbols and rituals. The fact that Russians, Englishmen, Frenchmen, Germans and Americans, among others, used Freemasonry in their works clearly illustrates the spread of the Institution across national borders. Freemasonry, then, was an accepted part of society and the general populace recognized its outward, and perhaps supposedly esoteric, trappings.

From both of the aforementioned points a third factor can be deduced. By the 18th century the parochial mysticism and secrecy of Freemasonry had evaporated. The pedagogical domain of the Craft had been invaded as education became more widely available to the masses and exposés of the Institution, a la Prichard, were widely published. The philosopher's stone remained undiscovered. Operative Masonry gave way to the speculative and esoteria was minimized. In short, moral humanitarian factors began displacing the vocation pragmatism. Freemasonry became available to the enlightened of all vocational pursuits. Once the Craft entered this new phase of evolution, it entered the public domain and became the object of careful scrutiny. From this scrutiny came reference points that various authors utilized in order to elaborate upon themes they developed.

In truth, even the most diligent scholar and careful author could only speak to the aura surrounding the Institution. The emotional ties associated with the Craft could be captured, in part, by a Kipling or Burns, but the moral thread so carefully woven through the Fraternity, tied by ritual and participation, could not be experienced vicariously. Literature could bring the spirit of the Institution to the uninitiated, but only a superficial knowledge could be gained. In essence, the richness of Freemasonry's literary references can be fully understood only by Freemasons. What if Sherlock Holmes could identify an arc-and-compass breastpin? The importance of the passage focuses not on the pin, to the Initiated, but rather to the symbolism of the pin. The greater implications, to the profane, went unnoticed. *The Prince of India* observed the working tools of a Master Mason, but no explanation of their functional utility was forthcoming. Kipling could speak of a Lodge of Instruction or a nebulous "Third Degree," but what understanding could the non-Mason bring to these terms?

The Institution of Freemasonry has been experiencing increasing visibility in all forms of written expression since the 18th century. It is clear, in retrospect, that the 18th and 19th centuries were turning points for the establishment of Freemasonry as a viable social institution in the Western World. The growing social status of the Craft is evidenced by the increased use of its outward signs in popular literature. Such literature chronicled a new age in Masonic awareness and activities.

Footnotes

[1]*The Man Who Would Be King*, Rudyard Kipling. Doubleday and Company. New York, New York.

[2]"Banquet Night," *Debits and Credits*, Rudyard Kipling, Doubleday and Company, New York, New York.

[3]"Mother Lodge," *The Seven Seas*, Rudyard Kipling,
Doubleday and Company, New York,
New York.

[4]*Kipling*, John Beecroft, Doubleday and Company, New York, New York.

[5]*The Prince of India*, Lew Wallace, Harper and Row. New York, New York.

[6]*The Cask of Amontillado*, Edgar Allan Poe, *The Oxford Anthology*, edited by William Benet and Norman Pearson. Oxford Univ. Press, New York, New York. 1938.

[7]*The Red-Headed League*, A. Conan Doyle, Harper and Row Publishers, New York, New York.

[8]*The Mythology of Secret Societies*, J.M. Roberts, Secker and Warburg, London, 1972.

VI
Cherchez La Femme

If woman had no existence save in the fiction written by men, one would imagine a person of the utmost importance; very various, heroic and mean; splendid and sordid; as great as a man, some think even greater.
VIRGINIA WOOLF, 1929

One of the peculiar hallmarks of Freemasonry is the entrance requirements. Most Masons if they stop and reflect for a moment, can recall the Master reciting a brief list of individuals who were not permitted membership. A cursory glance about the lodgeroom will bring one obvious exclusion to mind. Women.

It is interesting to note that the law that prevents a woman from being made a Freemason is based on an interpretation of the old Lansdowne Manuscript of 1560, and not the actual wording contained therein. The manuscript stated that an Apprentice must be, "...of limbs whole, as a man ought to be." Whether the word "man" was a definite noun or a term to be interpreted in its generic sense was in some doubt one-hundred years later as the 1693 *Constitutions of the Freemasons* stated:

> The one of the elders taking the Booke, and he or she that is to bee made a Mason shall lay their hands thereon, and the charge shall be given. (1)

Some Masonic scholars believe that the word "she" mentioned in the 1693 constitutions was a misprint and should have read, "they," but they give no evidence or rationale for their reasoning.

In any event, the Charges compiled in 1723 by Anderson contained the first direct reference to women. It stated, "...the persons admitted members of a Lodge must be good and true men...no bondsmen, no women..." It is estimated that Speculative Masons simply adopted a custom inherited from their Operative brethren. Operative Masons accepted men who were hale, hearty and in possession of all limbs and members. Mackey writes:

> Woman is not permitted to participate in our rites and ceremonies, not because we deem her unworthy or unfaithful, or incapable, as has been foolishly supposed, of keeping a secret, but because on our entrance into the Order, we found certain regulations which prescribed that only men capable of enduring the labor, or of fulfilling the duties of Operative Masons, could be admitted. (2)

In this day-and-age of equal rights and emphasis on one's ability to perform a task regardless of age, sex or race, this restriction appears anachronistic, but one must remember Operative Masonry dates from a millennium past, and such concerns were indeed real and apparent.

It is, perhaps, only natural that the all-male fraternity would have challenges to its sexual exclusiveness. Have women ever been made Freemasons? History records several instances that appear to illustrate they have indeed, but under closer examination most accounts are sketchy, duplicative and not well documented. In retrospect, such assertions can be divided into two basic categories: in one case a woman had been detected observing a Masonic ritual and was given the degrees as a means to ensure her silence; and in the other case, women were admitted in a pre-planned aberration of Masonic rules and regulations. Stories falling in the first category seem to follow an identical pattern with only the names and peculiar circumstances being altered. Because of the pattern and sometimes fanciful reactions ascribed to the men present who had been surprised, there are doubts as to the validity of these accounts.

A good example of the first category is the alleged initiation of Elizabeth St. Leger, later known as Mrs. Richard Aldworth. Miss St. Leger, as one version of the story tells, sequestered herself behind a large grandfather clock and watched degree work being performed. Another version

Eng. by Robertson, Seibert & Shearman.   From an original Portrait.

HONORABLE MRS. ALDWORTH
The female Freemason.

has her peering through a brick she removed from the lodge room wall.

> The young lady, being giddy and thoughtless...made her arrangements...removed a brick from the wall...so placed, she witnessed the first two degrees in Freemasonry...(3)

In either event, she was caught, brought before the lodge and forced to undergo Masonic initiation to ensure her silence. To think that a Freemason would forcibly initiate anyone for any reason boggles the mind and stains credulity. Further, to assume that anyone would assume such a coerced agreement would bind a cowan or eavesdropper is totally ludicrous and indicates a naive faith that humbles reason!

A strikingly similar story is told by a Mrs. Bell, who actually published an advertisement in the January 6, 1770 edition of the New Castle *Weekly Chronicle*:

> This is to acquaint the public that on Monday, 1st inst., being the Lodge or Monthly meeting night of the Free and Accepted Masons of the 22nd Regiment...Mrs. Bell...broke open a door with a poker, by which she got into an adjacent room, made two holes through the wall, and by that strategem, discovered the secrets of Freemasonry...(4)

Boldly the advertisement proclaimed:

> So that any lady that is desirous of learning the secrets of Freemasonry by applying to that well learned woman, Mrs. Bell, ...may be instructed in all secrets of Masonry. (5)

Coil further notes that a similar event was related concerning an Edinburgh woman in 1772 who claimed to have witnessed Masonic degrees after secreting herself in a closet adjacent to the lodge room. Virtually identical stories are told of a Mrs. Catherine Babington who, in 1815, allegedly concealed herself in a room adjacent to a lodge and was discovered, and a Mrs. Beaton who allegedly hid in the wainscoting of a lodge room. (The wainscoting is the paneled wooden lining of an interior wall.)

Did these events really occur, or does the similarity in incident indicate tales woven from the fabric of imagination and fancy? No one will ever know. As Henry Coil so aptly put it, "The accounts are a good winter's night story."

The second category of stories bears closer scrutiny. Helene Barkoczy, for example, appears to have been regularly initiated in a Hungarian lodge, and the Grand Lodge of Hungary took action against all those who took part in her initiation. Further, the Grand Lodge declared the admission of Madame Barkoczy illegal and ordered her membership certificate to be confiscated if she ever attempted to present it to a regularly constituted Lodge of Masons.

Maria Desraismes was initiated in the French Lodge, *Les Libres Penseurs*, (The Free Thinkers) after the French Grand Lodge had refused earlier permission to do so. She later participated in numerous ceremonies of the Grand Lodge *Droit Humain*, or Lodge of Human Rights. The French Grand Lodge later treated Madame Desraismes and *Le Droit Human* as being clandestine.

One tends to lend greater credibility to accounts that include the official sanction and reactions of legitimate governing Masonic bodies. This is not to assert that all instances that fall into the aforementioned first category are fallacious, but they cannot be proved and in most cases defy common sense and logic.

It does appear that certain women, in direct contradiction to the Ancient Landmarks adopted by most jurisdictions, have witnessed Masonic Degrees and have been Initiated, Passed and Raised.

A pertinent question might focus on why contemporary Freemasonry continues to be an all-male Fraternity. What is the lodge's position on women?

> It does not follow, however, that women are to be kept out of any possible association with the Fraternity...Lodges in the first Grand Lodge...had feasts...to which wives, daughters and women friends were invited...gloves were sent to wives of a newly made member...[lodges] in London had...what was called a maiden's chambers [powder room], assembly room, and dining room exclusively for women...(6)

Contemporary Freemasonry, indeed, has many close ties to androgynous and/or adoptive rites and orders. Androgynous Orders, such as the popular Eastern Star, include men and women; Adoptive Orders are approved and recognized by the Masonic Order. Some Orders' names are easily recognized, i.e., Eastern Star, Amaranth, White Shrine of Jerusalem, Ladies Oriental Shrine of N.A., Job's Daughters, and Rainbow Girls. Other organizations, e.g., Orders of Beatitudes, Order of Joan D'Arc, Heroines of Jericho, Daughters of Isis, Daughters of Sphinx, and Daughters of the Desert are less known and their ties to the Fraternity less well identified.

The question of women and Freemasonry was addressed by Mackey:

> There are no women Freemasons, and never can be, and if Lodges in the future ever change the Landmark, it will mean they have ceased to be Masonic Lodges. (7)

This position is not untenable since it argues once a pure form has been altered, it ceases to be pure. Logically, this is so, just as Operative lodges were bastardized when they first accepted Speculative Masons. If Soroptimists accept males, they will no longer be the club they were originally intended to be, but will have developed into another organization. The same may be said of the Oddfellows, PEO Sisterhood, Knights of Columbus or any other organization that restricts its membership. Using Mackey's argument, however, once the Constitution of the United States was amended, or changed, it ceased to be the true Constitution of the United States.

The exact reason why women were not allowed into the operative masonic lodges undoubtedly focused on someone's determination as to their ability to carry out demanding physical labor. Although some might argue this was blatant sexual discrimination, a closer look at the requirements in light of their historical context does not support such a thesis. Men with certain physical handicaps or limitations were also prohibited from membership as were other categories of individuals whose presence on a work site was deemed to be a safety hazard. The early operative masons were attempting to set work codes not unlike moddern safety rules and regulations, to permit the construction to proceed without the threat of potential physical harm to the individuals banned or other workmen on the job. The continuation of such restrictions is simply an attempt on the part of modern speculative Freemasons to maintain, as close as possible, a direct uniform linkage to their ancient brethren.

The fact remains that throughout the ages, some women have been made privy to the so-called Masonic secrets. Perhaps some observed the ancient rites from positions of seclusion whereas others may have read some of the various exposes. In retrospect, such deviations from the accepted practices of the Craft have made no differences in Freemasonry's history, intent or purpose.

Footnotes

[1]R.L. Clegg, *Mackey's Revised Encyclopedia of Freemasonry*, p. 1113.
[2]*Ibid.*
[3]*Op. cit.*, p. 49.
[4]Henry Coil, *Coil's Masonic Encyclopedia*, p. 92.
[5]*Ibid.*
[6]R.L. Clegg, *Op. cit.*, p. 1405.
[7]*Ibid.*

VII
A Base Canard

R osicrucianism, alchemy, Elias Ashmole and Freemasonry: an unlikely combination that, in truth, never deserved to be placed in juxtaposition. Through a series of unwarranted conclusions, fanciful interpretations and outright fabrications, however, an alleged relationship was hypothesized, but never substantiated, that haunts Ashmole's memory and erroneously ties the Craft to quasi-mythological organizations. Such base canards have repeatedly plagued Freemasonry, but few are based on as flimsy evidence as the tales that attempt to connect Ashmole and Masonry to those who seek to turn lead into gold or other forms of quackery and fraud.

Elias Ashmole is another of a seemingly endless list of men whose footnote in Masonic history focuses on an oddity or peculiarity. Ashmole was a 17th century Englishman who apparently had an unquenchable thirst for knowledge, especially esoteric knowledges guarded by so-called secret societies. Perhaps it was this quest for hidden knowledge that caused him to petition Freemasonry; no one will ever know for sure, but in any event his personal diary records the following:

> 1646
> Oct: 16...I was made a Free Mason at Warrington, in Lancashire...[1]

This seemingly innocuous entry has earned Ashmole a type of Masonic immortality, as it is believed to be the first written record of the making of a Mason in England. Almost 36 years later, he further recorded:

> March, 1682
> ...I received a summons to appear at a Lodge to be held the next day at Mason's Hall, London...I was the Senior Fellow among them (it being 35 years since I was admitted.)[2]

Henry Coil interprets this citation as indicating Ashmole "...was not much interested in or attached to Freemasonry, having attended Lodge only twice in thirty-five years." A careful reading of the two passages, however, does not indicate a thirty-five year gap between lodge appearances, only that Ashmole was stating that on the occasion of his March, 1682, attendance, he had been a Mason for thirty five years.

Regardless of his attendance pattern, Ashmole was clearly interested in the esoteric, the mysterious, the so-called hidden knowledges. Married to a wealthy older woman, her death left Ashmole the money and the time to study whatever subjects interested him. His early interest in astrology led to other forms of antiquarian research. It was this pursuit of knowledge that led some to believe Ashmole was a Rosicrucian, but no such link has ever been developed. Indeed, the term "Rosicrucian" is somewhat confusing and misleading.

The Rosicrucians were not one single group, but rather a term applied to a collection of men and organizations that studied alchemy, astrology, Hermetic philosophy and a host of other esoteric fields.

> It would be sufficient to say here that when Elias Ashmole is called...a Brother of the Rosy Cross, it means only, within the measures of the evidence, that he was a student of alchemy, for there was a misdirected opinion in the past that every alchemist belonged to this (Rosicrucian) Order.[3]

Alchemy, in this essay, as related to Ashmole, Freemasonry and Rosicrucianism refers to a subject known as transmutation. Transmutation is an act or instance of changing or altering an object from one form to another, such as converting lead to gold or zinc to silver.

The tie between the disparate groups and men that become known as Rosicrucians and the Freemasonic organization comes from a series of coincidences. In the 18th century, for example, an advanced Masonic degree was created and named the "Rose Croix." This name is derived closely from the same etymological base as the word "Rosicrucian." Similarly, the Rosicrucians and Freemasons shared a number of symbols: i.e., the level, the circle, the

ELIAS ASHMOLE

Made a Freemason in 1646, this illustration is from
the picture in the Ashmolean Museum at Oxford,
England.

triangle, the globe and others. But, a Rose Croix Mason and a member of the collection of men known as Rosicrucians are not twin petals from the same flower. As Mackey points out, there is a definite divergence in the use of the symbols:

> These are [the symbols], however, interpreted, not like the Masonic, as symbols of virtues, but of properties of the philosopher's stone.[4]

The philosopher's stone is a mythical or imaginary stone, substance or chemical preparation believed to have the power of transmuting baser metals into gold. Alchemists have sought the philosopher's stone for aeons, but its existence has strangely escaped detection. Those who have sought such a "stone," have often joined secret societies hoping they would gain access to esoteric knowledge whereby they could discover the fabled transmutation process.

Although there is no direct linkage between the Rosicrucians and Freemasonry, a philosophical connection has been hypothesized that could foster a belief in such a tie. The Hermetic philosopher Isaac Holland once said:

> ...though a man be poor, yet may he very well attain unto it, the work of perfection—and may be employed in making the philosopher's stone.[5]

One scholar, Hitchcock, interprets Holland's remarks thusly:

> That is, everyman, no matter how humble his vocation, may do the best he can in his place—may love, mercy, do justly, and walk humbly with God; and what more doth God require of any man?[6]

If Hitchcock's interpretation is correct, then it is possible to draw a strong parallel between the Rosicrucian's philosopher's stone and the Freemason's Spiritual Temple. But, regardless of the correctness of the interpretation of that specific passage, it is indisputable that the Rosicrucian alchemists' search for a philosopher's stone was of a more materialistic base than the Freemason's quest for the Spiritual Temple.

When attempting to correlate the Rosicrucians with Freemasonry, the evidence is decidedly circumstantial. Men of stature in the 15th through 17th centuries, such as Ashmole, Abbé Pernety, and Baron Tschoudy, in their quest for knowledge and enlightenment, often joined several societies that held esoteric knowledge. Such multiple individual memberships led some to believe this had to be indicative of interlocking organizational affiliation. Similarly, when the Freemasons created the Rose Croix, such a coincidence only strengthened an already pre-formed opinion. The fact that all such societies practiced rituals designed to shield esoteria from the uninitiated appeared even more conclusive. The use of the same symbols appeared to be too great a coincidence to overlook.

Herbert Poole, editor of *Gould's History of Freemasonry*, draws three meaningful conclusions when discussing possible linkages between the various Rosicrucians and Freemasonry:

1—That while there was an abundance of astrologers, alchemists, charlatans and visionaries of all kinds who seemed to have pursued their hobbies without let or hindrance, there was no organized society of any sort...

2—That there is no trace of any sect of Rosicrucian...philosophers.

3—That there is no trace, as far as any remaining evidence is concerned, that the Freemasons were in any way connected with any one of the above...they had not amalgamated with any of the supposed Rosicrucian or Hermetic fraternities...[7]

Those who link Freemasonry with the Rosicrucians possess only a superficial knowledge of either society. Circumstantial evidence led to unwarranted conclusions. The fact that individuals held such views is, perhaps, not surprising given the atmosphere and state of knowledge existing in the 17th century. What is less understandable, however, is the fact that as the 21st century draws near, some people still cling to this misconception; a misconception spawned some 400 years earlier.

Marcel Proust once said, "The opinions we hold...are in no sense permanent...but are as eternally fluid as the sea itself." Perhaps it is time the erroneous tie between

Freemasonry and the nebulous Rosicrucian alchemists is recognized as a base canard, and given proper burial.

Footnotes

[1]Henry Wilson Coil, *Coil's Masonic Encyclopedia*, p. 72.
[2]*Ibid.*
[3]Arthur Waite, *A New Encyclopedia of Freemasonry*, p. 373.
[4]Robert Clegg, *Mackey's Revised Encyclopedia of Freemasonry*, p. 878.
[5]*Ibid.*, p. 773.
[6]*Ibid.*
[7]Herbert Poole, ed., *Gould's History of Freemasonry*, pp. 104-105. vol. ii

VIII
Mozart and Freemasonry

Wolfgang Amadeus Mozart, as most school children learn, was an Austrian composer and musician born in 1756 and died 35 years later in 1791. In retrospect, as with many revered historical figures, his posthumous reputation far exceeded his earthly rewards. Today his name invokes memories of operas, arias, and other musical compositions, but during his life he had to seek out patrons in order to earn a living and in death he received a fourth class pauper's burial. Mozart's reputation as a composer is unparalleled, but his tie to the Masonic Fraternity is not as well known. If the tie is mentioned at all it is usually in reference to *Die Zauberflote* (the Magic Flute). In actuality, the tie between composer and the Fraternity is much deeper than this solitary opera, and a closer examination reveals much about the character of Mozart the man, and 18th century Austro-German society.

It can be safely asserted that among all the intellectual, moral and altruistic forces of the late 18th century, none enjoyed a more prominent position than Freemasonry. European society was fraught with so-called secret societies, but it was Freemasonry that grew, prospered and achieved the zenith of its expression. The intellectual giants of this era found themselves drawn to the confines of the Masonic temples as a natural magnet where they could discuss the affairs of the day in privacy and safety.

Perhaps the finest examples of the inherent attractiveness of Freemasonry to the great minds of the 18th century are the Austro-German lodges that claimed Mozart, Goethe, Frederick the Great, and other prominent men as members. These lodges were more than simple edifices where Masonic ritual could be performed. The lodge *Zur Neugekronten Hoffnung* (New Crowned Hope), for example, could almost be equated to a fine private club. It boasted

WOLFGANG AMADEUS MOZART

two large auditoriums, various science laboratories, large lodge rooms and countless smaller lounges for intimate conversations and private gatherings. The lodge's tasteful appointments focused on rare art and handsome antique furniture. Men gathered to argue, debate and discuss the political and economic issues that could not be safely vocalized in public.

Wolfgang Mozart lived in the midst of the political turmoil of the 18th century and Freemasonry had a pronounced influence on his life. Not only did he incorporate the precepts of Masonry into his personal life, but many of his musical works reflected his commitment to the Craft, most notably the *Magic Flute*. Although the *Magic Flute* is Mozart's most famous Masonic-related composition, many of his works alluded to Masonic principles or were actually written for the lodgeroom. *Gesellenreise* (1785) is ostensibly a social song, but it was expressly written for the opening or closing of lodge. *Kleine Freimaurercantate* was composed on November 15, 1791 and first performed a few days later at the dedication of a new Masonic temple. Other works were written specifically for tenor voices and male chorus and suggest a Masonic influence as do their lyrics and attendant symbolism.

The Magic Flute, however, stands apart as Mozart's total Masonic effort. The essence of the opera focuses on moral virtue and adherence to personal convictions. Many passages from this opera were taken directly from Austro-Germanic ritual or allude strongly to it. For example, in the 22nd scene a reference is unmistakably given to a symbolic journey: "Oh endless night hast thou no breaking? When dawns the day mine eyes are seeking?"

More specifically, the *Magic Flute* contains a passage where a man seeking admission into a private society is asked a series or preparatory questions. Before gaining admission into this society, in this case a priestly sect housed in an Egyptian temple, the candidate's guide or sponsor is asked: Is he "...virtuous? Can he be silent? Does he love his fellowman?" After answers in the affirmative the guide is asked, in essence, by what further right or

benefit does the candidate expect to gain the enlightenment he seeks. Sarastro, the guide answers, "Still more, he
is human." Later, in the third scene, the orator, who stands
parallel to the Master of a lodge, asks the candidate whether he wishes to continue or turn back because "...one
more step and it will be too late."

It must be pointed out that many critics of the dialogue
in this opera are critical of the seemingly disjointed and
awkward construction of the phrases. Since most of the
critics were/are not Freemasons, the use of Masonic ritual
is lost and whereas their criticisms are technically correct,
the fuller meaning of the opera escapes their grasp. It has
been hypothesized that only a Mason, or one who has acquired a knowledge of 18th century Austro-Germanic
Masonic ritual, can fully comprehend the *Magic Flute*.

The music itself, aside from the dialogue, also sug-
gests Masonic overtones. The overture, with its pounding
rhythms, alludes to craftsmen pounding on rough stones.
There are many three-fold sequences of 8th note phrases
and, in the trial by fire section of the opera, the sobbing vio-
lins create a serious mood that underscores the solemnity
of the Masonic ritual.

Some critics feel that the *Magic Flute* has far more importance than simply a great opera with Masonic significance. They feel that the *Magic Flute* strikes to the quick
of man's ancestorial existence, exposing, if you please, the
primordial elements in mankind's collection of ancient
heritage. They see themes of death, resurrection and other
concepts and philosophies common to ancient mysteries
being brought forward in the *Magic Flute*. The opera, they
argue, has Masonic themes only because Freemasonry
concerns itself with those elements that have long concerned man in his quest for theistic expression and inquiry.

Whatever the comprehensive level of the observer, or
the mental gymnastics one chooses to play when cri-
tiquing the opera, virtually all critics agree that the *Magic
Flute* is the greatest example of Mozart's consummate dra-
matic gift. Neither *Cosi Fan Tutti* nor *La Clemenza di Tito*
reveal the strength and depth of this composer. The zenith

of his abilities, it can be argued, was revealed in the Masonic opera, the *Magic Flute.*

Why did Freemasonry play such an important role in Mozart's life? The answer to that question goes far beyond the pale of this limited essay, but certain broad conclusions can be drawn. First, Mozart was an extremely altruistic person and he saw in Freemasonry a certain commonality with his own personal philosophy. His letter to his father in 1781 when Leopold was seriously ill, perhaps dying, alludes strongly to Freemasonry and its hidden secrets. Also to be considered are the social considerations, that is, during the later 18th century the great intellectual and artistic minds of Austro-Germanic society found the Masonic lodges a convenient means of social intercourse. Mozart's friends, especially the composer Haydn, were Freemasons. Social and philisophical considerations were undoubtably intertwined, perhaps inextricably interwoven, as Mozart committed himself to the Craft.

Even in death Mozart's Masonic ties were quite evident. Although he had a fourth class, or pauper's burial, at his wife's insistence, there were Masons present to honor him. Later, during a series of eulogies presented in his Lodge, Ignaz Alberti spoke the following words:

> He was in life good, mild and gentle,
> 　A Mason of good sense and open heart.
> The Band is severed now, may Masons' blessing
> 　Accompany him, bright and keen.

It is incorrect to assume that Freemasonry abandoned Mozart at his death as has been popularly repeated. Familial requests prevented any other type of arrangements.

Mozart's influence on Masonic music far exceeded his own labors. Franz Liszt, Alexander Zemlinsky, and Theodor Veidl all composed Masonic pieces. Richard Wagner was much interested in the Craft, but was apparently dissuaded from joining by personal commitments and obligations. Nonetheless, selections from his works appear to have Masonic influence, in particular *Parisfal.* Almost two centuries later such Masons as Jean Sibelius, John Philip Sousa and Irving Berlin have continued Mozart's rich tradition.

To this day Wolfgang Amadeus Mozart remains somewhat an historical enigma. Noted for his nationalism and patriotism, his altruistic nature and love of Masonic principles, he has also been accused of being anti-Semitic and a libertine. As with all historical figures, much can be said, but too little can be authenticated. All mortals have moral and spiritual flaws and to expect perfection is to expect the impossible. It has been said that to be a good Mason you must be a good man. What constitutes goodness is often subjective and predicated upon societal interpretation. Mozart, history records, thought himself to be a conscientious Mason and devoted a large part of his life to exemplifying Freemasonry.

IX
Phoenix or Ashes?

In ancient Greek mythology the Phoenix was a bird that lived 500 years. The Phoenix was reputed to be a magnificent creature whose beauty and graceful flight defied description. In addition to its beauty and grace, it had one other exceptionally outstanding characteristic: at the end of 500 years it would immolate itself on a pyre. From its own funeral ashes, however, it would reappear as a reborn youthful bird, destined to live another 500 years before the fiery death and rebirthing sequence would then occur. The Phoenix was symbolic of beauty and goodness that never died, but instead rose from its own ashes to live, again and again.

As the world rushes blindly toward the 21st century, it becomes apparent that mankind studiously examines its ashes, but we tend to ignore the Phoenix that brought us to today. We tend to dwell on our failings, the sensational and the morbid, but we shrug off our accomplishments as if such actions were to be expected and not worthy of notice or comment. This is a dangerous trait for it can cause us to overemphasize the negativism that forever hounds man. And, like Sisyphus, be forever doomed to an exercise in futility. Psychologists have examined a phenomenon they label the "self-fulfilling prophecy," that is, a tendency toward the eventual realization of something once people believe a result is inevitable. Child psychologists have long known that a youngster who is constantly told he is bad, incompetent, clumsy or dumb, will soon develop characteristics paralleling the image others project of him. The reverse is also true, as the Broadway show *My Fair Lady* so aptly described. Such a phenomenon has long been known and was the focus of the historical tale of Pygmalion.

A very serious question arises: Do American Freemasons tend to study our ashes and forget the Phoenix that brought us here today? Do we tend to dwell excessively on the problems confronting the Craft and deny the strengths of the qualities that permeate the Fraternity? Let us examine the following passage from the magazine, *The Michigan Freemason*:

"In our jurisdiction we have many lodges which do not seem to thrive as they ought. The meetings are not attended by the members as they should be, and while all confess that they respect the institution of Masonry, and believe its principles to be very good, and well calculated to perfect and elevate mankind, yet they wonder that so little interest is taken in the Order by the membership in their particular locality. The meetings of these Lodges are neglected, and the officers grow disheartened, and all join in wondering why it is so few are interested in an institution which we are free to admit is a good one."

Our present situation sounds desperate and undoubtedly we are doomed to certain extinction. Oops, wait a minute. Let us examine the date of *The Michigan Freemason* from which the passage just cited was taken. It is March, 1872. That's correct. The passage that to many ears seems so descriptive of today's situation, the passage that forecasts gloom and doom, was written over 100 years ago!

We often forget that Freemasonry is not an isolated social organization, but is composed of men who live and work in a much larger society. The composition of the Craft mirrors a greater society. To be sure, the average age of a Freemason in some locales is fast moving past 60, but let us not forget this merely reflects demographic trends in all aspects of life. The baby boom of the 1940's is now in mid-adulthood. Adult part-time students now outnumber traditional college-aged students across the nation. Throughout the land universities are adopting the attitude, "smaller, but better." Rote numbers have never indicated quality. Freemasonry should be concerned with quality not quantity.

The realization of dwindling membership is not unique to Freemasonry, nor to this era of Freemasons. We tend to forget that Masonry, as it is organized and practiced in the western world today, is simply not that old of an institution with a history of a large percent of eligible men holding membership. The first Grand Lodge was not formed until

THE PHOENIX

1717 and although many Masonic zealots attempt to trace modern ritual to King Solomon and beyond, prudent research cannot extend modern history far beyond the *Regius Manuscript*. Every organization, over a period of time, will develop a natural cyclical pattern of membership peaks and valleys. Likewise, at various times the average age in a Masonic lodge will shift. Those who predict a dire return for Freemasonry based on the number of white-haired heads on the sidelines at Blue Lodge or at the Grand Ldge are, perhaps, too myopic. Whereas all are entitled to their opinions, the chance of developing a damaging self-fulfilling prophecy is readily apparent. This is not to assume a Pollyanna approach of closing one's eyes to the obvious, or ignoring negative trends, but rather to caution the doomsayers to take a broader look at Freemasonry. To be sure, any vibrant social organization must make changes to adjust to constantly evolving social trends; even the Constitution of the United States has been amended dozens of times, but such growth and change in Freemasonry can and will occur.

Those who gloomily examine the Masonic ashes without realizing the Masonic Phoenix serve the Craft no good function. Such soothsayers, intentionally or not, create a form of hypothetical anxiety that is not constructive to the future of Freemasonry.

Management studies have shown that successful people have built strong positive views of their capabilities. Organizations are mirror-images of their memberships' abilities and attitudes. An organization that is filled with negativism and forecasters of doom will surely project that image to the outside world. This is not a newly discovered phenomenon, but a fact that has been recognized for decades. In 1917, for example, the hotel magnate E.M. Statler sent a memorandum to his subordinates that said, in part:

> "From this date you are instructed to employ only good natured people, cheerful and pleasant, who smile easily and often...If it is necessary to clean house, do it! Don't protest. Get rid of grouches, and the people who can't keep their tempers, and the people who act as if they were always under a

burden of trouble and feeling sorry for themselves...Hire pleasant, cheerful people..."

Statler concluded:

"I believe that a majority of the complaints in a hotel are due more to the guests' state of mind than to the importance of a thing about which he complains."

Without the benefit of modern studies, hotelier Statler seized upon a prime psychological principle: attitude precedes performance! This is yet another variation of the aforementioned self-fulfilling prophecy.

Charles Garfield, a professor at the University of San Francisco Medical School, developed a list of six keys to success that successful people have in common. The six keys are:

1. Successful achievers are able to transcend their previous level of accomplishment.
2. They never feel complacent about what they have already accomplished.
3. They enjoy what they are doing for the sake of doing it.
4. They tend to solve problems and forge ahead rather than taking time to assess blame.
5. They take risks only after carefully studying the situation and contemplating the worst possible consequences.
6. They are able to "rehearse" future actions by thinking them through and visualizing situations.

Perhaps the most gratifying part of Garfield's study focuses on his assertion that the six keys to success can be learned. Organizations can adopt these keys as well as individuals.

Point four is especially german to Freemasonry, that is, it does no good to assess blame for the sake of blaming. Constant recall of the good old days will not make the past reappear; indeed, the good old days were seldom as good as they are remembered. In 1982, the Grand Lodge of California took a bold innovative step in publicizing Freemasonry by inserting colorful tabloids in newspapers throughout the State that profiled the Craft, its history, purposes and activities. This was a bold task taken after careful consideration that transcended previous efforts. In Oregon, a television show was produced that explained away the ill-cloaked half-truths that have surrounded Freemasonry, and gave a clear, logical exposure of the Fraternity. Only time will tell the worth of such projects, but irrespective of membership gains, such projects are repudiations of the nay-sayers and a commitment toward positive proactive steps!

Freemasonry should be looking to the future, not bogged down in acrimonious fact finding or finding warmth and security in a glorious past. Too often Masons tend to revel in the past without planning for tomorrow. Contemporary society seems to believe that change-induced problems are unique to this era, but in the 1770's Adam Smith wrote: "there is always a deal of ruin in the nation." Generations in the past have been beset with as much, if not more, disorder and confusion than we are now. Our love of the past can be explained in a variety of ways, but perhaps the most salient reason focuses on a natural uneasiness that all people feel when confronting the unknown. There is no easy way to overcome this problem, but there are definite steps one can take to minimize the pull of inertia on the subconscious mind. Tom Lawrence presents a concise approach to solving problems.

> ...start to visualize what kinds of steps might be most productive in putting the problem or situation into a more acceptable posture. Think of these steps as a scenario that will lead toward a given favorable conclusion. Take the process apart, then put it back together again, always leading toward...an ultimate conclusion.

> Next, try to see yourself deeply involved in handling these steps. Most important, can you visualize how you will look and feel and think when you are on top of the problem...

> It is difficult, complex, but attainable still in programming the human computer toward given goals.

> Many years ago a philosopher said: "...whatever your field of enterprise and whatever your position in it, remember the force of the human mind. So, you should never declare you are that which you do not wish to be."

We have always known — yet we sometimes fail to remember — that the world largely accepts us at our own estimate of ourselves. There is a good reason: It is because we almost always live up to our own estimate of ourselves.

It is important to consider the Phoenix in its entirety and not dwell on its funeral pyre. One should not reject the potential negative effects of a dwindling membership, but to dwell on that single issue is exceedingly myopic. The future should be regarded as an ally, not an enemy, and plans for creating a smaller, but better Craft, can develop.

The Royal Bank of Canada recently published a newsletter that capsulizes the thrust of this article. The newsletter said:

"The best hope for society lies along the same lines, in the systematic study of future probabilities and the development of contingency strategies in advance to deal with them. Change itself has provided the tools for this in the form of new technologies, techniques and academic skills. 'By making imaginative use of change to channel change, we can not only spare ourselves the trauma of future shock,' wrote Toffler (author of *Future Shock*), 'we can reach out and humanize future tomorrows.' We now have it in our power to anticipate change, or to resist it. Which shall we choose?"

Indeed, which shall we, as Freemasons, choose? Shall we anticipate change, or resist it? History reveals the dinosaur resisted change...and where are they now? Which shall we choose?

X
Washington Afield

*"In traveling: a man must carry
knowledge with him, if he would
bring home knowledge."*
SAMUEL JOHNSON
1778

George Washington was a truly remarkable man: soldier, patriot, statesman, and politician. He was one of a rare breed of men who answered history's call and, like Cincinnatus, responded in a decidedly positive manner. If Shakespeare was correct, that some men are born great, some achieve greatness and some have greatness thrust upon them, then Washington was indeed an anomaly. Whereas he was not born with great stature, he achieved greatness as he was thrust into prominence.

In some regard, history has not been totally kind to Washington. To be sure, it is a singular honor to be known as the Father of one's country, but the folklore that has become part and parcel of every elementary schoolboy's remembrance of Washington has, in some ways, obscured some very real and very meaningful contributions to American government. Most Americans remember President Harry Truman thwarting General Douglas MacArthur's attempt to upstage him at a meeting in the Philippines with Truman demanding the proper respect be shown to the office of the presidency. Few historians note, however, that Truman had a precedent. In 1789, or almost two hundred years before Truman and MacArthur faced each other, President George Washington performed a like feat when Governor John Hancock of Massachusetts attempted to force a breach of proper etiquette. Washington, as a general, is often pictured in the prow of a rowboat crossing the Delaware or kneeling in prayer at Valley Forge, but his military expeditions in the Revolutionary War far exceeded the personal military exploits of any president who followed him. Whereas, the stories of a little boy who cut down a cherry tree, who would not tell a lie, who married a woman named Martha...and probably had false teeth made from wood, are an integral part of the warp and woof that constitutes American folk history; the real George Washington, his deeds and exploits, remains less visible and less well-known.

Travels

George Washington's life as a traveler reveals a great deal about this singularly unusual man. He traveled extensively in the American West, the New England area, and the South. Surprisingly, Washington never once traveled to either England or France, nations that played such prominent roles in his life. Indeed, his only foreign travel was to the Caribbean Island of Barbados when he accompanied his brother, Lawrence, who was suffering from tuberculosis.

Before delving into the travels themselves, various items of interest stand out concerning Washington as a sojourner. First, Washington was not the quintessential tourist. Archibald Henderson, in writing about Washington as a traveler, stated:

> Washington was no ordinary tourist, reveling in travel for its own sake, but a traveler with a purpose. He always had an objective; and concerned himself very largely with recording the events of the journey or describing the country with reference to that objective.[1]

Not only was Washington extremely business oriented as he traveled, but his logs, journals, or diaries of those trips reflect his preoccupation with recording only usable data.

Henderson further records that Washington "never unpacked his soul in a journal" and carefully "husbands space, and meticulously records only the most interesting of external events." It appears that when Washington did engage in subjective journalism, it was through the eye of a surveyor, which was his profession, or as an agriculturist, his other vocation, or as a fledgling capitalist, which he was to become. Washington was, a careful reading of history reveals, a competent businessman who utilized his travels to gain a greater understanding of what the land had to offer, both as a natural resource as well as a means of transportation. Washington's diary of his last western journey carries the following line that underscores his pragmatism: speaking of the West, he wrote, "It is to open a wide door, and make a smooth way for the produce of the West to pass to our markets before the trade may get into another channel..."

One of Washington's first recorded ventures into the hinterlands occurred in 1748 when, at the age of sixteen, he accompanied Lord Fairfax into Virginia as the surveyor of Fairfax's holdings beyond the area known as the Blue Ridge. Although Washington was only sixteen years of age, he had already assumed a position of some responsibility. One should be cautioned, however, about placing too great an emphasis on his youth because in 1748 a sixteen-year-old was considered a man and not viewed in the same perspective as a sixteen-year-old lad in 1984! The maps Washington drew on this expedition which are, according to most cartographers, "...models for the accuracy of the plot, the clearness of the description, and the neatness of the chirography." Evidently, Washington was a highly competent surveyor which, in retrospect, was a desirable trait for someone destined to map the future of a new country. Finally, Washington's journals recount meetings with German-speaking settlers deep in the American forests as well as a party of Indians returning from a war. Washington describes the Indians by their dancing and gives a good description of their musical instruments. It is instructive to realize Washington's detail of observation over items that might easily have been overlooked by a less attentive chronicler.

Between the years 1753 and 1784, Washington traveled extensively through Virginia, Maryland, Ohio, and contiguous regions. It was during this period (1754) that Washington was captured at Fort Necessity and, obviously, later released. Washington's capitalistic nature was revealed in his land dealings in Ohio where (1770) he acquired thousands of acres. Washington acted on his own behalf as well as being agent for soldiers who had served in the ill-fated Fort Necessity venture. Washington's last journey to the West occurred in 1784. Because of his activity and involvement in the war, Washington undertook his western tour not as a capitalistic land acquisition swing, but rather to inspect and consolidate his current holdings. He wished to reestablish his rights to land he owned. Washington was a careful man and, in personal finances, he might be considered fiscally conservative. After the Revolutionary War, a prominent French official invited Washington to visit France, but he graciously declined referring to his personal financial affairs.

As might be expected, Washington found it expedient to travel rapidly and often between 1775 and 1781. His itinerary consisted of locations now made famous by the Revolutionary War: Philadelphia, New York, Boston, New Haven, Springfield, Hartford, West Point, and many, many others including, of course, Yorktown, Virginia. Washington's Revolutionary War travels are too extensive to be detailed in this article. Suffice it to say that his travels in this six-year period were of necessity and not dictated by personal preference or choice.

Presidential Tours

As President, Washington made three separate tours through all the thirteen original states. As in his younger years, Washington's diary is, as Henderson stated, "...a model of circumspection, strongly objective, and reminiscences of his own past experiences are conspicuously absent." It was on his so-called "Eastern Journey" of 1789 that the little known "Hancock Incident" occurred. The incident, in capsulized form, focused on Governor Hancock's effort to force the President to call upon him, as Governor, when Washington visited Massachusetts instead of having a State's Governor call upon the President. Whereas this may appear a trivial matter in 1982, one must remember that in 1789 the Union was quite new and such protocol was extremely important. The precedent established would, to a large degree, greatly influence such important concepts as states' rights and the importance of the federal government. Washington held fast and refused to call upon Hancock. Hancock, after a series of excuses, finally visited the President. The precedent was established and the dignity of the office preserved for future generations.

Washington undertook yet another journey after North Carolina ratified the Constitution in 1789 that had him visit various locations in Virginia, the Carolinas, and as far south as Georgia. He was well received and elaborately entertained. A variety of anecdotal materials is available concerning these travels. The hazards of travel in the immediate past revolutionary era were readily apparent. Washington wrote of traveling by dusty horse-drawn carriages, of chilly ferry crossings, and somewhat inadequate lodgings. Perhaps the most telling recollection, however, was written after a trip to Richmond on April 12, 1791:

> In the course of my enquires...I cannot discover that any discontents prevail amongst the people at large, at the proceedings of Congress...
> [They are] favorable towards the Federal Government, and they only require to have matters explained to them in order to obtain their full assent to the measures adopted by (the government)...[2]

I am afraid that if Washington were to reappear today, travel the same route, and make inquiries amongst the same population, his conclusions might be radically different.

Masonic Travels

The story of George Washington as a Mason has been told, retold and undoubtedly embellished over the past two hundred years. Whereas this brief work does not pretend to chronicle such a history, it is an interesting sidebar to Washington's military and presidential travels to focus on some of his Masonic activities during the same period. It is interesting, for example, to see that President Washington valued his Masonic relations and continued them over a large geographic region.

Without attempting an exhaustive coverage, it can be pointed out, for example, that in 1782 Washington's presence is recorded in the minutes of Solomon's Lodge in Poughkeepsie, New York. Three years later, in 1785, Washington wrote in his diary:

> Received an invitation to the funeral of...the oldest inhabitant of the town; I went-up and walked in procession as a free mason.[3]

When Washington was inaugurated as President in 1789, the Grand Master of New York Masons administered the oath. In 1790, during his southern travels, he reached Georgetown, South Carolina. After a meeting with a member of Prince George's Lodge, Washington wrote:

> Gentlemen...I am much obliged by your wishes and reciprocate them with sincerely assuring the fraternity of my esteem, I request them to believe that I shall always be ambitious of being considered a deserving Brother.[4]

Washington's sentiments toward the Craft were mutually received. When he traveled on to Savannah, Georgia, Grand Master George Houston is recorded as saying:

> Happy indeed is the Society...that can boast of [George] Washington as a brother.[5]

Hugo Tatsch in *Freemasonry in the Thirteen Colonies* capsulized Washington's reception:

> A tour of the Southern states was made by President Washington in 1791. He was the recipient of many Masonic honors in various cities.[6]

In 1793, Washington laid the cornerstone for the nation's capitol in Federal City, now known as Washington, D.C., using the appropriate Masonic ritual and ceremony.

Even a cursory examination of the foregoing travel illustrates Washington's continued involvement with Freemasonry while involved in government travels. It is revealing of his character and his affection for the Craft, that be it New York, Virginia, South Carolina, Rhode Island, Georgia, or other locations, he valued and exercised his Masonic relations.

Fellow-citizens and Brothers;
of the Grand lodge of Pennsylvania

I have received your address
with all the feelings of brotherly affection
mingled with those sentiments, for the
Society, which it was calculated to excite

To have been, in any degree, an
instrument in the hands of Providence
to promote order and union, and erect upon
a solid foundation the true principles of
government, is only to have shared with
many others in a labour, the result of
which let us hope, will prove through
all ages, a sanctuary for brothers and
a lodge for the virtues. —

Permit me to reciprocate your
prayers for my temporal happiness,
and to supplicate that we may all
meet thereafter in that eternal temple
whose builder is the great Architect
of the Universe

G Washington

GEORGE WASHINGTON'S RESPONSE TO THE GRAND LODGE OF PENNSYLVANIA

The Grand Lodge of Pennsylvania organized a committee to
form an address to be presented on St. John's Day,
December 21, 1796, to honor the retirement of President
George Washington from public service. This address was
delivered to Washington at his residence.

Retrospect

George Washington was, indeed, a remarkable man, one of the few men in history whose stature actually grows as truth is extracted from fiction. His travels, whereas not as exciting as perhaps to the casual reader as Gulliver's travels, give accurate insight into our first President, not only as a man, but also as a manager... in this case, the manager of a fledgling new enterprise identified as the United States of America.

The scope of his travels cannot be construed as extensive and many of his contemporaries outstrip Washington in raw mileage logged, but of more importance was the quality of his travel: its purpose and the results. His accurate journals and diaries have provided a wealth of information for the diligent scholar. His handling of early issues of protocol and etiquette established precedents followed today, 250 years after his birth. Oliver Goldsmith, in his oft cited poem, "The Traveller," has penned these lines that capture the essence of Washington as a sojourner through new born America.

> Where'er I roam, whatever realms to see,
> My heart untravelled fondly turns to thee.
>
> ....
>
> Such is the patriot's boast, where'er we roam,
> His first country ever is at home.

Footnotes

[1]Archibald Henderson, *Washington the Traveler*, p. 119.
[2]*Ibid.*, p. 129.
[3]William McCamant, "George Washington, The Mason," Research Lodge of Oregon's *Masonic Papers*, 1932-35, Volume 1, p. 7.
[4]*Ibid.*, p. 12.
[5]J. Hugo Tatsch, *Freemasonry in The Thirteen Colonies*, p. 80.
[6]*Ibid.*, p. 141.

XI
Freemasonry and the Ancient Mysteries: A Nebulous Connection

*"Mysticism is, in essence, little
more than a certain intensity and
depth of feeling in regard to what is
believed about the universe."*
BERTRAND RUSSELL
1917

With no outrageous pun intended, the Ancient
Mysteries are quite mysterious to most people,
including contemporary Freemasons. There are, of
course, innumerable theories that hypothesize linkages from one or another Ancient Mystery to the Fraternity,
but there cannot be developed, with absolute certainty, a
direct casual relationship or an uninterrupted transfer of
esoteric information from any one single Mystery to Freemasonry. Isabel Cooper Oakley, who attempts to develop
such a relationship in the book, *Masonry and Medieval
Mysticism*, capsulizes her efforts thusly:

> As researches into its history are pursued, it appears...that
> the Masonic movement, to state it generally, was a sort of
> broad, semi-mystic and largely moral movement, worked
> from certain unknown centers, and not generally known
> basis.[1]

This is, obviously, a rather open-ended assessment that
falls quite short of establishing any link whatsoever. It is
instructive, when pursuing this theme, however, to define
the terms being used. Although Oakley could not develop a
linkage between Freemasonry and the Ancient Mysteries,
what exactly is meant by the term, "Ancient Mystery"? The
The term, "Ancient Mystery" is, in itself, mystifying;
conjuring images of Merlin-type magic, esoteric and sequestered secret knowledges. Even the names of such
Mysteries: Osiric, Mithraic, Adonisian, and Eleusinian, for

example, sound quite exotic to the Occidental ear and, to some, offer the possibility of possessing secrets somehow lost to modern man. In reality, the Ancient Mysteries are not so mysterious once they are understood in terms of their *raison d-etre* and once their structure is understood, the cosmetic link to contemporary Freemasonry is clarified. Once again, what is meant by the term "Ancient Mystery"?

> Each of the Pagan gods . . . had, besides the public and open, a secret worship paid to him, to which none were admitted, but those who had been selected by preparatory ceremonies called Initiations. This secret worship was termed the Mysteries.[2]

The various Ancient Mysteries had certain features in common with one another. They were all, for example, funereal in nature. There was a death and resurrection theme in each Mystery. The candidates for admission passed through a series of degrees before reaching full membership in the Mystery. The initiation rites were conducted in the dark; sometimes in a cave, a darkened room, in a dense forest at night, or in some other circumstance where the successful candidate could eventually be brought to enlightenment. The candidates were also subjected to dangers in their initiation process, dangers so real that pain was common and death was not beyond the pale of possibility.

Compare the structure of the Mysteries, without details of their esoteric practices, with that of Freemasonry. Freemasonry has the Hiramic theme that is funereal in nature and there is a subordination of degrees through which a candidate must pass with the eventual goal of spiritual enlightenment. In Speculative Masonry, the dangers encountered by the candidate are symbolic and pose no threat to an Initiate, but in Ancient Operative Masonry the initiation may indeed have carried more than symbolic meaning.

The esoteric nature of the Mysteries is repeated in Freemasonry. The Mysteries required an oath of secrecy from the candidate that was enforced by the severest sanctions. Because the Mysteries were associated with deity worship, violation of their secrets was considered a sacrilege and punishable by death. Such penalties were not taken lightly, as witnessed by a statement attributed to Horace: "I would forbid," he said, "that the man who would divulge the sacred Rites of mysterious Ceres from being under the same roof with me, or from setting sail with me in the same precarious bark." Candidates who successfully passed their initiation into a Mystery were forbidden to discuss their initiation, the knowledge they had obtained or even the symbolism parochial to that particular Mystery.

Mackey points out the similarity again, between Freemasonry and the Ancient Mysteries, when discussing the concept of secrecy.

> These virtues [secrecy and silence] constitute the very essence of all Masonic character; they are the safeguard of the Institution...The same principles of secrecy and silence existed in all ancient Mysteries...When Aristotle was asked what thing appeared to him to be most difficult of performance, he replied, "To be silent."[3]

It is easy to see why learned individuals attempted to find a relationship between specific Mysteries and Freemasonry. The parallel construction of the disparate Mysteries to the Fraternity's structure is extensive. In retrospect, however, this should not be particularly astounding since the structure adopted by the Mysteries is an ideal method to keep secrets: religious, philosophical, or trade, privy to a chosen few. The penal structure in ancient times would be as effective, or perhaps more so, than contemporary threats of professional disbarment or license removal to modern keepers of esoteria. What better way to ensure craft secrets, such as construction, than by forming a society that not only restricts membership, but also presents real penalties for revealing those secrets? Accordingly, the more meaningful the secret, the greater the possibility of having penalties envoked. Consequently, as Freemasonry moved from Operative to Speculative, the penalties for revealing Masonic secrets became less real and more symbolic.

Perhaps the strongest link between the Ancient Mysteries and Freemasonry is not to be found in tracing the esoteric knowledge contained in a specific Mystery to the Craft, but rather in examining the structure of the two types of societies.

> ...this is not because the Masonic Rites are a lineal succession from the ancient Mysteries, but because there has been at all times an aptness of the human heart to nourish a belief in a future life, and the proneness of the human mind to clothe this belief in a symbolic dress.[4]

Further, to nourish these beliefs, all used symbolism and scenic representation to emphasize their beliefs. There is one area of potential similarity that should be of concern to all Freemasons. It is reported that there was a drastic change of admission requirements in the Mysteries, for a variety of reasons, as their membership declined. When there was no dearth of potential initiates, the Mysteries elected only those men whose lives were irreproachable, men who had spotless reputations and whose public lives and personal activities would withstand close scrutiny. By the fourth century, however, membership began to dwindle, and the leaders of the existing Mysteries decided to lower their standards and accept as initiates men who did not meet previous rigid standards.

> The vile and the vicious were indiscriminately...admitted, Their [Mysteries] character was changed...peddling priests...[sold] to every applicant...that which had been refused to the entreaties of a monarch.[5]

Finally, in 438 A.D., or 1,800 years after they first appeared in Greece, Theodosius ordered all Mysteries abolished. Some Mysteries lived on, covertly, such as the Mysteries of Mithras, but eventually disappeared as valid and vibrant organizations.

What conclusions, if any, can be drawn that connects Freemasonry to the Ancient Mysteries? Oakley cites Robert Gould's tripartite theory concerning the creation of Freemasonry:

> It [Freemasonry] may have come down to us:
> 1. Through a strictly Masonic channel
> 2. Through the Rosicrucians
> 3. Through a variety of defunct societies whose usages and

customs have been appropriated, not inherited, by the Freemasons.[6]

Irrespective of claims to the contrary, there is no logical or historically traceable connection that shows a direct lineal connection between any Ancient Mystery and contemporary Freemasonry. Freemasonry may have adopted forms and symbols of the Mysteries, but it is illogical to claim a direct inheritance.

> As far as known, Freemasonry is not and never was connected with the Ancient Mysteries in any way. The theory that it was, seems to have been urged sometime, by devotees out of excessive imagination...Very little analytical logic went into the development of the Ancient Mystery theory of Freemasonry.[7]

Such theorists that still claim lineal connection between the Ancient Mysteries and Freemasonry would do well to heed the words of Giambattista Vico, written over two hundred years ago: "Imagination is more robust in proportion as reasoning power is weak."

Footnotes

[1]Isabel Cooper Oakley, *Masonry and Medieval Mysticisms*, p. 31.
[2]Robert Clegg, *Mackey's Revised Encyclopedia of Freemasonry*, p. 689.
[3]*Ibid.*, p. 920.
[4]*Ibid.*, p. 691.
[5]*Ibid.*
[6]Oakley, *Op. cit.*, p. 35.
[7]Henry Coil, *Masonic Encyclopedia*, p. 433.

XII
Cause Celebre:
The William Morgan Affair

The fabric of American history has always revealed the thread of Freemasonry. At times, as during the battle for independence and the early years of the new Republic, the Craft played a dominant role in creating and defending American ideals and institutions. At other times, the Masonic thread has been more subtle, nearly hidden in the folds of our national past. Always, however, the Craft has been a part of the warp and weft of America, a unifying thread that has exerted a significant force on the development of the Nation. An interesting example of this fact is the Morgan Affair which led to the creation of America's first third-party movement.

If the name of William Morgan is mentioned in Masonic circles, the most probable reaction is one of mild evasion. William Morgan in 1826 authored an exposé of the secret rituals of Freemasonry entitled *Illustrations of Freemasonry*. History tells us that Morgan was abducted from a location in New York, disappeared and was never found. He was presumed by many to have been silenced by Freemasons who did not want his book to be published. The story of the William Morgan Affair is interesting, but in point of fact, the greatest impact that Morgan had on American history is only peripherally related to the actual content of his book. The far-reaching effect was one of great political importance in the development of political parties in the United States. Before delving into the greater ramifications of William Morgan's disappearance, it is necessary to explore the reasons why he became a *cause celebre*.

William Morgan is somewhat an enigma in Masonic history. There is no record of Morgan ever being Initiated, Passed and Raised as a Master Mason. Yet, an examination of Western Star Chapter No. 35 in LeRoy, New York, reveals

Morgan petitioned for the degrees of Royal Arch Masonry in 1825 and was Exalted to the Royal Arch in May of that year. It is known that he visited a Symbolic Lodge in Batavia, New York, several times and that he was also among a group of men who received advanced instruction from the New York Grand Lodge's Grand Lecturer, Dr. Blanchard Powers. At this point in time, Morgan appeared to reach the zenith of his Masonic career. A decision was made by New York Masons to start a Royal Arch Chapter in Batavia, and Morgan joined in the effort, but for reasons unknown to this day, his name was struck from the roll. Whether this prompted him to develop anti-Masonic sentiments, or whether he needed money, no one will ever know; but within one year he was attempting to find a publisher for his exposé on Freemasonry.

The knowledge of the impending publication of Morgan's book caused great consternation among New York Freemasons who were offended by his conduct. Repeatedly, Morgan went from tavern to tavern boasting of the progress he was making on the book. Legitimate Freemasons felt that Morgan had duped them, and now they were about to suffer the consequences.

Several attempts were made to stop the publication of the book, but difficulties focused on the fact that Morgan had already acquired partners, and he no longer controlled the very book he authored! Morgan had allied himself with Daniel Miller, a printer who evidently had taken the Entered Apprentice Degree, but advanced no further. Two other men provided the financial backing needed to subsidize the printing.

Several events now occurred that indicated certain men were growing impatient with passive attempts to halt the book's publication. Miller's print shop was set afire. He claimed the Masons did it to stop the book's printing; the Masons claimed Miller set the fire himself in order to get publicity for the book. Later, criminal charges were brought against Miller on unrelated events in an effort to incarcerate him and prevent further work on the book. These charges were dismissed. A second fire broke out at Miller's

A SUPPOSED PORTRAIT OF WILLIAM MORGAN

shop. Then, out of the blue, Morgan was arrested on charges of theft.

At this point the story of William Morgan becomes muddy and unclear. What is clear is that Morgan was released from jail on September 12, 1826. Outside the jail was a waiting carriage that Morgan entered. It is not certain whether he entered the carriage willingly or unwillingly. Morgan's whereabouts can be traced to Fort Niagara, but there are no reliable accounts as to his presence after September 19, 1826. He disappeared.

There are a plethora of stories as to what happened to William Morgan. The Freemasons who could be identified as being in Morgan's company from Batavia to Fort Niagara claimed Morgan accepted a sum of money in return for leaving New York, never to return, and resettling in the Canadian wilderness. Anti-Masonic groups claimed the Masons murdered Morgan in retaliation for revealing secret Masonic rituals. In reality, no one knows what really happened to William Morgan. The fact is, however, that his disappearance caused Freemasons who lived through the 1827-1840 period to experience many difficult moments. In addition, the William Morgan Affair developed an historical perspective that went far beyond the actual events of that era.

Long Range Implications

The Morgan Affair was to spawn the appearance of America's first national third party and the holding of the Nation's first national nominating convention. The appearance of this third party was to set a pattern for future third party efforts, a focus at first on a specific issue and later a more broadly based platform.

The anti-Masonic sentiments that grew so rapidly after Morgan's disappearance clearly illustrate a latent animosity for the Fraternity that existed prior to 1826, even as early as the immediate post-Revolutionary War days. Certain religious groups such as the Quakers, Mennonites, Moravians, and even the Lutherans opposed membership in any so-called "secret society."

On January 13, 1827, an anti-Masonic convention was held in Seneca, New York. Within a month 11 more conventions were held, and an anti-Masonic newspaper was started in Albany. Anti-Masonic sentiments grew geometrically. Not surprisingly, membership in the Fraternity began to drop. In less than a decade, between 1827 and 1835, representation in New York's Grand Lodge dropped from 127 lodges to only 41. Every lodge in Vermont surrendered its charter and, obviously, the Vermont Grand Lodge ceased to function. The anti-Masonic atmosphere dwindled membership throughout New England and even traveled as far west as Michigan.

Political Opportunists

The anti-Masonic sentiments that swept through the population provided a natural catalyst for political opportunists.

Many historians believe that if America had enjoyed a strong two-party system in the post-Morgan Affair era, the Morgan incident would not have achieved the prominence it did and would have been relegated to only a minor footnote in history. Unfortunately, for the Freemasons of that era, the Federalists and Anti-Federalist dichotomy of John Adams' day had all but disappeared. George Washington was, in essence, a man above politics as related to political parties and their daily activities. Washington's influence, however, pulled Adams into office, and that precipitated a struggle between Adams and Alexander Hamilton. The subsequent election of Thomas Jefferson (a Republican-Democrat) over Aaron Burr destroyed the Federalists' control of government. More importantly, Jefferson's election and subsequent election of his successors, effectively muted two-party rule. Various divisions appeared within the party, but nothing to rival the earlier political split.

So, when William Morgan disappeared and anti-Masonic sentiments receiving widespread popular support, many young intelligent men saw a political vehicle for developing their own political futures. This is not to imply that all men who supported the anti-Masonic campaign were simple opportunists, for many did believe in the cause, but rather a marriage of opportunity and commitment was created that afforded many men the chance to develop their own political lives and oppose the politicians in power.

In any event, on Independence Day, 1828, the factions opposing Freemasonry held a State convention in LeRoy, New York. This was not their first foray into politics, however, because in 1827 the Anti-Masonic Party enjoyed stunning, and surprising, success in the New York State legislative elections. They elected seven candidates in the senatorial districts and almost elected an eighth, until, to the chagrin of the Anti-Masonic Party leaders they found they had nominated a Mason for the State senate! They quickly threw their support elsewhere and defeated their previously endorsed candidate.

The events at the LeRoy convention led some anti-Masonic Party members to believe they were being duped or used. Through political maneuvering it was decided not to nominate a candidate for Governor, but rather to wait and see who was nominated by the Adams' party convention in Utica two weeks later. The announced reason for such a maneuver was to see if an acceptable anti-Masonic candidate would be nominated and the combined support of the two groups would prove to be a formidable voting bloc.

In Utica the gubernatorial nominee was not a Freemason, but neither was he a vociferous anti-Mason. The extreme anti-Masons were disappointed so they met a second time and nominated their own candidate for Governor. To their embarrassment and chagrin, their candidate refused the nomination and accepted the nomination of the Adams' party for Lieutenant Governor. The Anti-Masons, persistent to the end, met a third time and nominated Solomon Southwich for Governor. He finished third in a three man race. Although the Anti-Masonic Party lost the governorship, they made substantial gains in both the State house and senate. In 1831, at Baltimore, Maryland, the anti-Masonic Party nominated William Wirt, a Virginia lawyer, for President. He won seven electoral votes and enough of the popular vote from Henry Clay, allowing the re-election of Andrew Jackson to the Presidency in 1832.

Ironically, the success of third parties in America has always led to their demise, because larger groups see the success they enjoy and try to absorb them into their structure. Third parties are usually one or two issue oriented, and elected officials find themselves making decisions on a veritable plethora of matters, and not just the issue they rose to prominence debating.

The Anti-Masonic Party set this pattern for all third parties that followed. By the mid 1830's, Anti-Masonic Party members were opposing one another on domestic as well as foreign issues. The solidarity that brought them into office was slowly being ruptured, and by 1840 the movement, as a single issue party, was tired and spent. Slowly the Anti-Masonic Party members began to be absorbed into a larger political alliance, the Whig Party, that was not born from a negative orientation, but focused instead on solving social issues of the day.

In retrospect, the role American Freemasonry played in the development of third party efforts to capture the White House is not, one might say, totally favorable, yet American political history is richer for the William Morgan Affair, the resultant third party and the precedents established by this splinter group. Once again the extent of the pervasive nature of Freemasonry is demonstrated through this seemingly innocuous "footnote" on American history.

XIII
Three Feet East, Three Feet West, Three Feet Perpendicular

The date 1717 is generally associated by contemporary Freemasons with the founding of the first Grand Lodge in England. It is generally assumed that the formation of the Grand Lodge was a consolidation move designed to develop a healthier and sounder Masonic organization and such a merger was welcomed and encouraged by all Freemasons in England. This perception would be incorrect. There were several Masonic organizations that did not want to form a new all-encompassing Grand Lodge and whereas they were not always inimical to the new Grand Lodge, they preferred to go their own separate ways. Still other fraternal orders were either created or continued their existence, and these orders saw themselves as rivals or direct opponents of the Grand Lodge.

Henry Coil, in a *Comprehensive View of Freemasonry*, lists seven such "rival" orders. He mentions the Philo-Muscae et Architectural Societas Apolloni; Appollonian Masons; Modern Masons; Antediluvian Masons; Honorary Masons; Ral Masons; and the Scald Miserable Masons.[1] Of the aforementioned orders, the Antediluvian Masons were among the most interesting, and their history is a microcosm of the confusion and misinformation that has permeated Masonic organizations throughout history and has continued well into the 20th century.

The word "antediluvian" is derived from the Latin base, i.e.; *ante*, meaning "before," and *diluvium*, meaning flood. Antediluvian Masonry, therefore, would translate as Masonry that existed before the flood. What flood? In this case, the flood referred to is the Biblical flood that destroyed all life on earth except that which was saved by Noah and his ark. Antediluvian Masonry purported to be an ancient form of Masonry that preserved the true and ancient forms of ritual and, therefore, was directly polarized to the changes in the Fraternity being perpetrated by the new Grand Lodge and other orders.

Briefly, the Antediluvians believed that prior to the flood the true Masonic secrets were permitted to be preserved by God in such a manner that the impending deluge would not destroy them. There are two basic legends, somewhat divergent, but in reality quite similar.

One legend states that Lamech had three sons and one daughter. The sons were the founders of three sciences: Jabel founded geometry, Jubal founded music and Tubal Cain founded smithing. A daughter, Naamah, founded weaving. The secrets of these four "sciences", and thus the basis of Freemasonry, were inscribed on two pillars. One pillar could withstand the ravages of fire, the other could withstand the ravages of water. After the flood, Hermes supposedly found the pillar that withstood the flood, transported it to the building site of the Tower of Babel, and thus allowed Masonry to be passed on to future generations.

Dr. George Oliver relates a similar, but slightly different tale. Oliver tells us that: "Enoch, as Grand Master, practiced Freemasonry with such effect that God was moved to make known to him some peculiar mysteries. Among these secrets was the sacred Word that continues to this day to form an important part of...(Masonry.)"[2] Enoch also had two pillars built, one of brass, the other of stone, on which he engraved the elements of the liberal sciences, including Freemasonry. Later, Enoch gave the reigns of government over to Lamech, along with the secrets of Freemasonry. Lamech eventually passed them to Noah. After the flood, the pillar of brass was no where to be found, but the pillar of stone, with its messages intact, was located. Thus, to this day, the secrets of Freemasonry are available through Antediluvian Masonry.

Although the legends are not identical, the essence of the Antediluvians' existence is focused on their claim that certain Masonic secrets were made known to man before the flood and were preserved in such a way that those who practiced Antediluvian Masonry would be exposed to such secrets. Other forms of Masonry did not possess access to these secrets and, therefore, should not be believed or trusted. Since the lodges that consolidated to form the Grand Lodge were not Antediluvian lodges, the forms and rituals expressed in their Masonry was a bastardization of true Antediluvian Masonry.

How clear the anti-Grand Lodge stance of the Antediluvian Masons became in the decade after the formation of the Grand Lodge can be discerned from an announcement that appeared in a London newspaper in 1726, alerting Antediluvian Masons to an impending Lodge meeting:

> "To all Masons who have been made after the Antediluvian Manner...That there will be a Lodge held...tomorrow... there not being Brethren enough assembled the last year to make a true and perfect Lodge.
>
> There will be several lectures on Ancient Masonry, ...and how and after what Manner the Antediluvian Masons form'd their Lodges, shewing that Innovations have lately been introduced by the Doctor and some of the Moderns, with their Tapes, Jacks, Moveable Letters, Blazing Stars, and, to the great Indignation of the Mop and Pail.
>
> There will likewise be a Lecture...that neither the Honorary, Apollian, or Free and Accepted Masons know anything of the matter; with the whole History of the Widow's son...
>
> By order of the Fraternity,"
>
> Lewis Giblin, M.B.N.[3]

Coil, and others, believe that Antediluvian Masonry was probably organized more to ridicule the new English Grand Lodge and the accompanying rituals, than to conduct meetings of its own. A close examination of the newspaper announcement tends to support this contention.

First, it is stated that the previous year's meeting was cancelled due to an insufficient number of members needed to constitute a valid lodge. It strains credulity to believe that an active vibrant order would meet only once a year, and then have that meeting cancelled due to a lack of members in attendance! Similarly, the tyler of the lodge was announced to be a Gormogon. This is astounding because the Gormogons were a rival fraternal organization that actively opposed Freemasonry. There are several theories as to the origins of the Gormogon Order, several focusing on Papal ties, the Jesuits and the infamous Chevalier Ramsay. Irrespective of the order's origins, a London newspaper of September, 1724, printed a notice of a Gormogon meeting that included the following line: "...nor will any Mason be received as a Member till he has renounced his Novel Order and been properly degraded."[4] It is difficult to imagine a serious Masonic Order, even a rival Grand Lodge Masonic Body, that would use an announced antagonist to the Fraternity as a tyler for its annual communication unless the purpose was to accent the polarization between the Antediluvians and the Grand Lodge!

The Antediluvian announcement contained many references to terms both familiar and unfamiliar to contemporary Freemasons. Tape, Jacks, Moveable Letters, Knuckles, Wrists and an interesting phrase: Three Foot East, Three Foot West, and Three Foot Perpendicular. All such terms are rather mysterious to contemporary Freemasons whereas others, such as: Parallel Lines, Blazing Star, Middle Chamber, and the Widow's son, are quite familiar. The author of the announcement was obviously well versed in terms used by Grand Lodge Freemasons as well as Antediluvian Masons. Or could such mysterious terms and phrases have been used simply to whet the interest of other Freemasons and strengthen the Antediluvians' claim that their lecture would present information, "...that neither the Honorary, Apollian, or Free and Accepted Masons know anything of..."?

The announcement plainly ridicules the new Grand Lodge, symbolic Freemasons, Dr. Desagulier and others who supported the new Masonic Order. This writer even finds the name signing the newspaper announcement to be somewhat ironic. There may indeed have been an Antediluvian Mason named Lewis Giblin, but the irony of such a coincidence is astounding. Giblin, sometimes spelled Giblim, is a significant word in Freemasonry. Mackey points out that "...where Giblim is supposed to be synonymous with Freemasons."[5] Mackey further states that the Giblim or Giblites, are mentioned in the scriptures as assisting Solomon's and Hiram's builders to prepare the trees and stones for building the Temple. The man's first name, Lewis, needs little explanation. In the English system of Masonry, from which the announcement's author would have been familiar, the word "lewis" is found on the Tracing-Board of the Entered Apprentice Mason and is the symbol of strength. Thus, the man's name translates Masonically as "strength in Freemasonry," especially that original Masonry associated with Solomon. A fitting name for a man representing an organization that claimed to have pure ties to ancient Freemasonry. Perhaps the name is a coincidence. Perhaps not.

In retrospect, the Antediluvian Masonic Order, and other Masonic or quasi-Masonic organizations that did not meld with the Grand Lodge in 1717, were the dying gasps of individualized or idiosyncratic Masonry. Within 100 years the various rituals and degrees practiced by these orders became non-operative or at least non-competitive with the Masonic organization dominant in the world today. Certainly an altar may be placed in a different location in an English lodge than a lodge in Wisconsin, or the wording slightly different in a F. & A.M. jurisdiction than in an A.F. & A.M. jurisdiction, but the differences are slight compared to the schisms separating Antediluvian Masonry, for example, from Scald Miserable Masons, or between other factions that did not unite with the Masonic bodies that formed the first Grand Lodge.

Undoubtedly, many of the Masonic or quasi-Masonic Orders that died, or are now inoperative, possessed interesting and meaningful degrees and rituals, degrees and rituals that are, perhaps, forever lost. It is consoling to note that contemporary Freemasonry and its concordant bodies have enough history, philosophy and ritual work to keep the most diligent researcher or scholar, as busy as his time and energy permits. But, wouldn't it be interesting to know what was meant by, "Three feet east, three feet west, and three feet perpendicular"?

Footnotes

[1]Henry Coil, *A Comprehensive View of Freemasonry*, p. 78.
[2]Robert Clegg, *Mackey's Revised Encyclopedia of Freemasonry*, 1921 edition, p. 154.
[3]Henry Coil, *Masonic Encyclopedia*, p. 52.
[4]*Ibid.*, p. 285.
[5]Clegg, *Op. cit.*, 1966 edition, p. 403.

XIV
Scald Miserable Masons

"Parades should be classified as a Nuisance and participants should be subject to a term in prison. They stop more work, inconvenience more people, stop more traffic, cause more accidents, entail more expense . . ."

WILL ROGERS
1924

Until Will Rogers made his now famous statement concerning parades, it was generally assumed everyone loved a parade. Indeed, Masonic history is replete with parades or processions that called attention to Freemasonry and the men who associated themselves with the Order. Gould's *History of Freemasonry* lists 26 separate references to Masonic processions.[1] A strange quirk of history, however, reveals that perhaps the most famous procession associated with Masonry was conducted by a group of men who undoubtedly had no Masonic ties. Calling themselves "Scald Miserable Masons," these men etched their existence into history by organizing two parades, in 1741 and again in 1742, that were designed to mock Freemasonry and hold the Fraternity up to public ridicule. One might ask, why anyone would want to achieve such a devious objective.

In 1741, the English Grand Lodge was only 24 years old and the schism that had divided Freemasons against one another concerning the consolidation of English Freemasonry had not yet completely healed. Remnants of non-Grand Lodge Masonic bodies as well as rival fraternal organizations and anti-Masonic groups still existed and occasionally surfaced for brief moments of public notoriety. But, for the most part, the Grand Lodge of 1717 enjoyed solid, if not unanimous support of most English Freemasons.

Such support was exhibited in a variety of ways, including the creation of public Masonic processions. Henry Coil, in his *Masonic Encyclopedia*, emphasizes the fact that there is no mention of Masonic parades or processions prior to the formation of the Grand Lodge. "The first one to be recorded is that mentioned by Dr. Anderson in his *Constitutions of 1738* as having occurred on June 24, 1721..."[2] Anderson described the processional as consisting of various lodge officers who marched in "proper clothing and due form." He further reported that such processions occurred annually on St. John the Baptist's Day until the period 1741-1747.

Why such Masonic public processions or parades came into existence is difficult to determine with any degree of certainty.

> "The question has been often mooted, whether public processions...are or are not of advantage to the Order. Dr. Oliver was in favor of what he calls 'the good old custom', so strongly recommended and assiduously practiced by the Masonic worthies of the 18th century...to offer up their thanksgiving in the public congregation for the blessings of the preceding year."[3]

Others were not so favorably disposed toward such public demonstrations. Such Masonic processions must have irritated the non-Grand Lodge Masons and exacerbated anti-Masonic sentiments.

Perhaps the events of 1741 and 1742 are not so surprising when placed in the historical context of the Masonic schism of 1717 and latent anti-Masonic feelings that periodically surfaced in London during this era. What happened to bring the so-called *Scald Miserable Masons* to the public's attention was recorded in the March 20, 1741 issue of the *London Daily Post*.

> "Yesterday some mock Freemasons marched through Pall Mall and the Strand in procession; first went fellows on jackasses, with cows' horns in their hands; then a kettle-drummer on a jackass...(a) Grand Master and Warden; the whole thing attended by a vast mob..."[4]

The mock Masons called themselves *Scald Miserable Masons* which translates into the rather unpleasant title of

SCALD MISERABLE MASONS

Burlesque Procession of Scald Miserables in 1741
parading in front of the Apple-Tree Tavern.

"Scabby Miserable Masons." It is not known whether the group consisted of pranksters, rogues or sincere anti-Masons attempting to poke fun at the Fraternity. Whatever the intent, the reception they received from the real Freemasons, whom they encountered at the Temple Bar, must have been somewhat disappointing. The aforementioned newspaper article continued:

> "They [Scald Miserable Masons] stayed without the Temple Bar till the Masons came by, and paid their compliments to them, who returned the same with agreeable humor that possibly disappointed the witty contrivers of this mock scene."

The genuine Freemasons met the intended insults with grace and good humor and, evidently, took the sting away from the hoaxsters.

Another attempt at a mock processional occurred the following year, replete with shoe-cleaners, chimney-sweepers and other ridiculous pageantry. This second effort has been recorded for history by an engraver named Benoist. His work, entitled "A Geometrical View of the Grand Processional of the Scald Miserable Masons..." can be found in Clavel's *Picturesque History*.

The two mock Masonic processions may have been efforts to ascertain the general publics' sentiments toward Freemasonry. If this was the case, the organizers must have been sorely disappointed because the English upper-class appeared to be favorably disposed toward the Fraternity and did not view the processions with humor or favor. Historians record that the Prince of Wales discovered that his surgeon, a man named Carey, was one of the organizers of the *Scald Miserables*, and immediately discharged him!

The long range effect of the *Scald Miserable Masons'* processions occurred in a manner that was probably unexpected to the mock Masons. Mackey cites a Captain George Smith who stated that the second procession caused an order to be issued that discontinued all public parades of Masons on Feast days. In reality, five years elapsed between the two events. Coil does confirm Smith's assertion, but also points to the five year gap as an indication that the *Scald Miserables* did not succeed in halting genuine Masonic public processions. Was there cause and effect, or was there any causal relationship at all? History is mute on this point.

It is highly unlikely that the localized events of mid-eighteenth century London would have serious impact on American Freemasonry. In retrospect, it does not appear as if the *Scald Miserables'* actions crossed the ocean. Public processions occurred regularly into the 20th century, especially with the York Rite Masons and their Triennial Encampments. Their plumed hats and para-militaristic garb graced many parades and Easter services. In New York, in 1837, during the heated aftermath of the William Morgan Affair, the subject of a public Masonic procession did cause a schism in the New York Grand Lodge, but the controversy was totally independent from the events in London one hundred years earlier. In New York, one group planned a procession that was ordered cancelled, by the Deputy Grand Master, the day before it was to occur. The procession's organizers defied the Deputy and went ahead with the procession as planned. The ensuing rupture was not healed until 1850. Although the New York schism is interesting, the relevant point focuses on the existence of Masonic processions in the United States almost 100 years after they were banned in England. Even a cursory reading of Gould, Coil, *et. al.*, reveals many public Masonic processions throughout the Masonic world long after the *Scald Miserable Masons'* processions.

Contemporary Freemasonry sees few public processions other than funeral services and the laying of corner stones. The days of mass Masonic parades with men in gloves, aprons and other Masonic regalia appear to be minimal when compared to historical antecedents. The parallel between the meaning of the public processions of yesteryear and today is also very faint. If you are asked to conjure visions of modern Masonic processions one usually envisions Shriners clowning their way down children-lined streets, a band replete with Arabian costumes and red fezes, or motorcycle drill teams performing close order drills.

Freemasonry, like any other vibrant social organization, must change in order to stay meaningful. Perhaps the decline in public Masonic processions was inevitable as the Craft constantly seeks new methods of better serving its membership. Still, it is probably true that modern Masons will never see a procession such as the one that was reported in the *Freemasons Magazine* and *Masonic Mirror* of September 19, 1863:

"Friday, about 2 o'clock, the Grand Cavalcade of the Most Ancient and Honourable Society of Free and Accepted Masons, set forward...

The procession was as follows: A pair of kettle drums, 2 trumpets, 2 French horns, 4 hautboys, 2 bassoons, the 12 present stewarts in 12 chariots, the Master and warden... in one coach, the noblemen and gentlemen who have served in the Grand Offices...in one coach...the Earl of London's coach and six horses, empty, closed the procession.

The cavalcade proceeded through the Strand...to Fishmonger's Hall, where a very elegant entertainment was provided by the Stewarts. In the evening there was a grand ball for the ladies, and the whole was concluded with the usual magnificence and grandeua."[5]

Magnificence and grandeur! The *Scald Miserable Masons* antedated Goethe, otherwise they might have learned from his "Elective Affinities," namely: "There is nothing in which people betray their character than in what they laugh at." Laugh indeed, in this case it was the Grand Lodge that had the very last and very best laugh.

Footnotes

[1] R. Poole, *Gould's History of Freemasonry*, Vol. IV, p. 311.
[2] Henry Coil, *Masonic Encyclopedia*, p. 487.
[3] Robert Clegg, *Mackey's Revised Encyclopedia of Freemasonry*, 1966 edition, p. 808.
[4] Coil, *Op. cit.*, p. 594.
[5] Clegg, *Op. cit.*, p. 809.

XV
Captain Smith and His Traveling Lodge

*"Someone has to have the last
word. If not, every argument could
be opposed by another and we'd
never be done with it."*
CAMUS, *The Fall*

O n occasion, the recent history of Freemasonry
has noted a blazing star quite different than
that referred to in Masonic symbolism. In this case, the
blazing star refers to a person who appears, however briefly, and is brought into prominence for a period of time, and
then disappears without leaving a lasting or very mem-
orable impression on the Craft. Some of these blazing stars
have been reformers, or self-styled reformers, authors of
exposés, ritualists, or one-issue men of myopic propor-
tions. Joseph Cerneau was one such blazing star, Samuel
Prichard and Louis Claude Saint-Martin are other examples.
In some instances these men had a positive influence on
the Fraternity; in other cases the influence was decidedly
negative. In many cases the influence had no lasting effect
on Freemasonry, but illustrated man's propensity for self-
aggrandizement and ego gratification. Shooting across the
Masonic panorama in the 18th century was one such
blazing star, a man named George Smith. Smith is an
interesting character because he was responsible for two
small footnotes in Masonic jurisprudence. In order to
understand Smith, and his ability to affect Freemasonry,
one must first understand the English system of Traveling
or Military Lodges.

Traveling Lodges are also known as Military, Army,
Regimental, Foot or Ambulatory Lodges. Coil states:

"The warrant for such a lodge was issued to some officer,
usually a colonel of a regiment and accompanied that military unit wherever it might go..."[1]

The warrant referred to by Coil is a document from the
appropriate Grand Master authorizing the legitimate work
of a lodge. Without such a warrant no regular lodge could
exist.

The obvious intent of the existence of such Traveling
Lodges was to provide Masonic services to military men
who, by the very nature of their profession, might not have
access to regular permanent lodges. Coil further points out
that: "Membership was primarily limited to members of the
same regiment, and, in no event, were civilians supposed
to be admitted..." In addition to the Traveling Lodges in
the army, there have also been Sea or Naval Lodges.

It is important to recall the concepts surrounding the
existence of Traveling Lodges when later reading of Captain Smith's activities.

Captain George Smith was a career military man who
had been initiated into Freemasonry during a tour of duty
in Prussia. Smith was, evidently, a competent and respected militarist. After serving in the active army, he was appointed Inspector General of the Royal Military Academy,
in Woolwich, England, and later published two books, *The
Universal Military Dictionary* (1779) and the *Bibliotheca
Militares* (1783), on military subjects. From his professional
accomplishments and positions of responsibility, it can be
assumed that Captain Smith was a competent intelligent
man.

Mackey states that Smith was also a devoted Freemason and his record of service to the Craft illustrates a
deep involvement in Masonic lodge management. He
served as Master of his lodge at Woolwich for four years
and later, in 1778, he was appointed Provincial Grand
Master of Kent. In retrospect, it is apparent that Smith also
held a warrant for Royal Military Traveling Lodge No. 371
at this time. In 1780, Smith was appointed Junior Grand
Warden of the Grand Lodge of England. It is at this point a
controversy arose. Gould capsulizes the problem:

"At the ensuing Grand Feast, Captain George Smith was appointed Junior Grand Warden, though the Grand Secretary objected, that, being then Provincial Grand Master for Kent, he was disqualified for serving that office. Ultimately the objection was waived, Captain Smith offering to resign the Provincial Grand Mastership, should the union of both offices prove incompatible."[2]

Smith, and the Grand Secretary, a man named Heseltine, appeared to have established a pattern of conflict with one another. In this case, Smith's position was upheld, but it was, perhaps, a pyrrhic victory. The following November, Smith resigned the Junior Grand Warden's position and the Grand Lodge later adopted the regulation:

"...that it is incompatible with the Laws of this Society for any Brother to hold more than one Office in Grand Lodge at one and the same time."[3]

Thus, George Smith was responsible for the first of two Grand Lodge regulations that were created in a direct response to his action.

The cause of the animosities between Smith and Heseltine has not been recorded, but could very well have stemmed from another action by Smith that resulted in yet another Grand Lodge regulation!

In 1783, Smith learned that various Freemasons, who were prisoners at the King's Bench jail in London, had opened a lodge in the jail and were making Masons of their fellow prisoners. Smith, it may be recalled, still held a warrant for Royal Military Traveling Lodge No. 371, a warrant that was intended to be used only for military men and "...in no event, were civilians supposed to be admitted." Concerned that the degree work was being improperly administered, Smith assembled his Wardens and proceeded to the prison where they opened Lodge and initiated a certain number of prisoners. As might be expected, there was a hue and outcry from the Masonic hierarchy as well as rank-and-file membership. Smith and his Wardens were summoned before the Grand Lodge to explain their actions. To the chagrin and embarrassment of the Grand Lodge, they could find no prohibition against such activi-

THE

USE AND ABUSE

OF

Freemasonry;

A WORK OF THE GREATEST UTILITY TO THE BRETHREN
OF THE SOCIETY,

TO

MANKIND IN GENERAL,

AND TO THE

Ladies in Particular.

BY CAPTAIN GEORGE SMITH,

INSPECTOR OF THE ROYAL MILITARY ACADEMY AT WOOLWICH; PROVINCIAL GRAND
MASTER FOR THE COUNTY OF KENT; AND R. A.

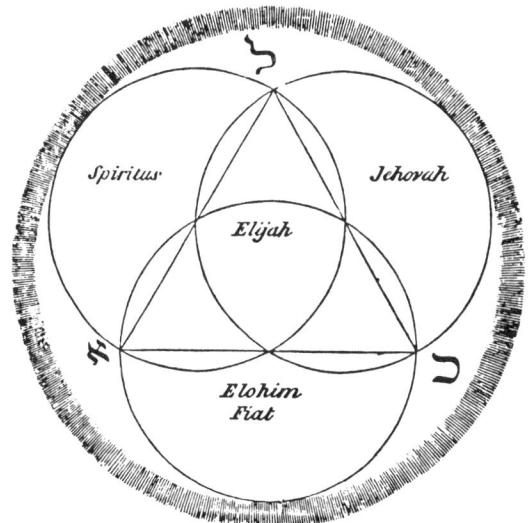

MACOY PUBLISHING & MASONIC SUPPLY CO.
45 - 47 - 49 JOHN STREET
NEW YORK, U. S. A.
1914

TITLE PAGE OF *USE AND ABUSE OF FREEMASONRY*

Smith's book orginially published in London in 1783 gained
popularity and was subsequently published in America in 1866.
The above shows the title page of Macoy's reprint of 1914.

ties. Thus, Smith made his second impact on the Grand Lodge as they adopted a resolution that stated:

> "...it is inconsistent for any Freemason's Lodge to be held, for the purpose of making, passing, or raising Masons, in any prison or place of confinement."[4]

Smith and his Wardens were also censured by the Grand Lodge and the next year the warrant for Royal Military Lodge No. 371 was dissolved.

Captain Smith had yet one more claim to Masonic fame, be it ever so small and perhaps inglorious. In 1783, Smith published a book entitled: *The Use and Abuse of Freemasonry: A Work of the Greatest Utility to the Brethren of the Society, to Mankind in General, and to the Ladies in Particular*. The book had been presented to the Grand Lodge for its approval and sanction, but official approval had been denied. Due to the constant state of agitation between Smith and the Grand Secretary, it should come as no surprise that his work was rejected. In any event, the Grand Lodge's official position was that the book made no significant contribution to Masonic literature. The Grand Lodge pointed to rapidly growing memberships and ample instruction that was available to substantiate their claim.

In retrospect, two views can be discerned on the topic. Some Masonic historians believe that Smith's book was indeed valuable and, aside from the twenty pages devoted to why women should be excluded, the work did open the way for the publication of Masonic literature. Mackey asserts there was a dearth of good literature available and cites the following passage from Noorthoude:

> "No particular objection [to Smith's book] being stated... the temptations to authorship have effected a strange evolution of sentiments since (1720), when even ancient manu-- scripts were destroyed to prevent their appearance..."[5]

Gould, on the other hand, calls the book "vapid and almost devoid of merit."

Irrespective of the merit of the book, Captain Smith was not dissuaded by the Grand Lodge's decision. He had the book published privately and it immediately sold out.

Evidently the public's opinion outweighed the Grand Lodge's evaluations.

Were the ill feelings that existed between Captain Smith and Grand Secretary Heseltine responsible for the Grand Lodge's refusal to sanction the book? With only secondary source material currently available, such a conclusion cannot be determined. It is obvious that Smith and the Grand Lodge sparred consistently during the early 1780s over a wide range of issues.

Behavioral specialists assert there are basically three types of conflict: episodic, chronic and cumulative. Cumulative conflict demands some type of action that resolves the underlying reasons for the problem. By 1785, the Grand Lodge, evidently, felt it had suffered all of the conflict it could handle vis-a-vis Captain George Smith. In that year Captain Smith was expelled from the Fraternity for "uttering an instrument purporting to be a certificate of the Grand Lodge recommending two distressed Brethren." No more is stated, no more is known. The identity of the distressed brethren, their cause and all other factors are hidden.

Smith has been described as being obstreperous, vapid and perhaps even sneaky, *i.e.* he looked for "loopholes" in Masonic law. Yet, no less a Masonic personage than Dr. George Oliver described Smith as a man ". . . plain in speech and manners, but honorable and upright in his dealings, and an active and zealous Mason."[6]

It appears as if Captain Smith was a political animal who simply did not have the power or influence to successfully complete whatever design he set out to accomplish. The end result is clear; Smith's lasting impact on Freemasonry can be found in two Grand Lodge regulations that reform existing gaps in Masonic jurisprudence. The controversy over his book somewhat mirrors his own Masonic career, virtually a tempest in a teapot. He is a footnote in a much larger chapter. His blazing star shot across the Masonic horizon, then sputtered and faded from view. The fact that the discord was between two Masons only lends greater credence to Christopher Morley's observation that: "There is no squabbling so violent as that between people who accepted an idea yesterday and those who will accept the same idea tomorrow."

Footnotes

[1]Henry Coil, *Masonic Encyclopedia*, p. 417.
[2]Herbert Poole, *Gould's History of Freemasonry*, p. 68.
[3]Robert Clegg, *Mackey's Revised Encyclopedia of Freemasonry*, p. 949.
[4]Henry Coil, *Op. cit.*, p. 626.
[5]Robert Clegg, Op. cit., p. 949.
[6]*Ibid.*

XVI
Tricephalous Cerneauism and Clandestine Masonry

"A man has made great progress in cunning when he does not seem too clever to others."
LA BRUYERE
1688

If the word clandestine is used with a Masonic connotation, the usual mental imagery that accompanies it is fraught with furtive or illegal activities; men attempting to gain access to esoteric knowledge without the appropriate experiences. Indeed, even today lodges are opened with the reminder that the Tyler is to remain vigilant in the event cowans and eavesdroppers lurk in the darkness. Traditionally, a cowan has been defined as an operative mason who had not affiliated with the Fraternity, whereas an eavesdropper is self-defining. It is easy to understand why many Freemasons view a clandestine lodge composed of clandestine Masons being virtually a den of inequity, a room filled with dubious characters conjuring nefarious schemes. Correct? Well, not exactly. Henry Coil writes:

> [Clandestine]...means secret, hidden, private, or concealed, which might be said of many Masonic bodies. It also means underhanded, stealthy, sly, furtive, but many so-called clandestine bodies are quite open, aggressive, ambitious and eager to defend themselves.[1]

The term, in and of itself, does not carry a particularly negative connotation. It is instructive to note that at various times opposing Masonic bodies have labeled each other clandestine only to recognize the other at a later date, or even merge with one another.

There have been, however, examples of decidedly illegal activity in Masonic history. Two unrelated instances of clandestine activity, in the generic sense, occurred in the United States and occurred, oddly, within the last 150 years.

The first instance occurred in the early 19th century and focused not on Blue Lodge Masonry, but on the development and expansion of the then fledgling Scottish Rite in America and involved a man named Joseph Cerneau. "Cerneau was a product of the patent system by which the French degrees were at first disseminated in the Western Hemisphere...with much irregularity and occasional chaos."[2] Irregularity and chaos are key words because at the turn of the 19th century there was no single organized Masonic body in the United States that regulated or validated Masonic experiences. Post-colonial America experienced slow or poor communication channels and news concerning what had occurred in New York often took weeks, even months, to reach, for example, South Carolina. Joseph Cerneau came to New York from Cuba in 1806 claiming, at that time, to have the authority to confer a twenty-five degree system, or the Rite of Perfection. Cerneau was partially correct. He did have a patent, or permission, allowing him to confer the 4th through the 25th degrees, but only in Cuba; in fact, only in northern Cuba!

Irrespective of his legitimate authority, Cerneau, on October 28, 1807, opened in New York "The Most Puissant Sovereign Grand Consistory of Sublime Princes of the Royal Secret..." and made himself Sovereign Grand Inspector General. Cerneau, in a bit of free logic, awarded himself the 33rd Degree. It is acknowledged that Cerneau possessed the 25th Degree. In 1801, the 32 Degree system perfected in Charleston, S.C., moved the position of Prince Mason, or Prince of the Royal Secret, from its old slot as the 25th Degree to the 32nd Degree. Cerneau simply moved with the title change and, so to speak, went to the front of the class. Upon entering his Consistory he simply awarded himself the 33rd Degree to accompany his new title of Sovereign Grand Inspector General. His audacity went unchallenged. The fact that Cerneau "...exceeded [his] authority so easily and gracefully shows how credulous were Masons of that time, how avid they were to grasp at titles...and how little thought was given to Masonic regularity."[3]

Because of multiple Supreme Councils in the North, circa 1806, Cerneauism did not meet unified opposition and until the Great Compromise of 1867, it was virtually impossible for the best intended Mason to ascertain which body was regular or irregular. From Cerneau's creation of his Consistory in the early 19th century until the earliest 20th century, Cerneauism existed in various forms due to the constant splitting, merging and melding of Masonic and quasi-Masonic bodies. Some Masonic historians point to the date of 1919 as when Cerneauism finally gasped its last breath. Coil called Cerneauism a hydra which, when decapitated, grew several new heads. As late as 1886, Albert Pike referred to "tricephalous Cerneauism" and called the Thomson-Gorman Masonic Body the "Twin Bastards of Cerneauism."

In truth, many good men whose intentions were totally honest, associated themselves with Joseph Cerneau, or one of his created Bodies, under the false impression they were affiliating with a regularly constituted Masonic lodge. Unfortunately, even as Cerneauism was dying, another more crass scheme was being hatched that once again abused honest men's good faith and created yet another variation of clandestine Masonry.

On May 15, 1922, in Salt Lake City, Utah, three men were convicted of using the United States mail to defraud. Whether any of the three had even heard of Joseph Cerneau is problematical, but irrespective of their knowledge of Cerneauism, they perpetuated a hoax that created hundreds, perhaps thousands, of clandestine Masons.

Matthew McBain Thomson was a native Scot who came to American and affiliated with a regularly constituted lodge of Master Masons in Idaho. He later dimited from this lodge and formed, on his own, an organization he called the American Masonic Federation. Using a variety of sophistic arguments, he asserted that the United States was unoccupied territory, Masonically, due to the illegitimate nature of the existing Grand Lodges.

Thomson claimed he had a legitimate link to true Scottish Rite Masonry because he was from Scotland. Further, he and his chief assistants maintained he had the following of thousands of Masons and claimed countless positions of leadership in American and European Masonic Bodies; claims that went unsupported, but also unchallenged. To the uninitiated, his arguments sounded plausible and only a Freemason, or student of Freemasonry, could separate fact from fiction. None stepped forward to do so.

Why did Thomson and his confederates attempt to forge their own Masonic empire? It appears their motives were far from altruistic, but instead focused on the base: money! Simply stated, Thomson sold degrees. The usual fee for the Craft degrees was approximately $50, to move through the Scottish Rite to the 33rd Degree ranged from $135-$200. He also sold Shrine and Templar degrees.

Thomson and his associates probably could have enjoyed a long and prosperous business if they hadn't used the United States mail to obtain money and, thereby, come under the authority of federal laws.

The details of the prosecution are not as important as the judge's findings. Excerpts from his decision:

> Nobody can hear this evidence in this case without being convinced, absolutely convinced, that this thing has been fradulent from the beginning.

> I realize that some things can be proven by tradition, but tradition cannot exist with one man...no one who was skilled in the history of Freemasonry had ever met any such tradition so far as the record in this case is concerned...[4]

All of the principal parties involved were found guilty, sentenced to two years in prison and given a fine of five thousand dollars.

But, what of the thousands of men who paid their money and thought they were receiving legitimate degrees? And, why didn't regular Freemasons speak out?

Isaac Blair Evans, who was the United States attorney in Utah at the time of the trial postulated:

> Thomson also knew some things about regular Masons. He knew that they read very little about their own institution, and that, therefore, they are generally ill-informed in matters of Masonic history and law.[5]

In essence, Mr. Evans states that Freemasonry allowed the Thomson hoax to grow because Freemasons were ill-informed and, therefore, unable to launch a satisfactory defense.

Clandestine Masons are not necessarily men who, through devious methods, have overtly sought to circumvent the regularly established Masonic organizations and thereby gain esoteric knowledge illegally. In some historical cases the so-called clandestine Masons have been the unwilling dupes of shysters and hoaxsters who used the ignorance of men about the Fraternity for personal gain. James Thurber was right, you can fool too many of the people too much of the time.

Footnotes

[1] Henry Coil, *Masonic Encyclopedia*, p. 128.
[2] *Ibid.*, p. 120.
[3] Henry Coil, *Freemasonry through Six Centuries*, p. 196.
[4] R.I. Clegg, *Mackey's Revised Encyclopedia of Freemasonry*, pp. 207-208.
[5] *Ibid.*

XVII
From Mappa to Naperon:
The Evolution of the Masonic Apron

*"a pron (a pron) n. 1. A garment
worn over all or part of the front of
the body to protect one's clothes or
as a decorative part of a costume.
(originally* napron, *from Old French*
naperon, *tablecloth, from Latin,*
Mappa, *napkin.)"*
AMERICAN HERITAGE
DICTIONARY, 1980

Is there any other piece of Masonic regalia that is so readily recognized or identified with the Fraternity than the apron? By the same token, to the average citizen the sight of adult males, many in business suits or even formal evening wear, with white aprons secured about their waists, must be puzzling and, unfortunately, perhaps even comical. Most Freemasons can distinguish the various ways an Entered Apprentice Mason, a Fellowcraft Mason or a Master Mason is supposed to wear their apron, and probably be able to explain, in a fashion, the reasons why the aprons are white and made of lambskin; but the history of aprons in the ancient Mysteries and in organizations such as Freemasonry, however, is less well known. Mackey points out that the use of aprons "...or some equivalent mode of investiture, as a mystic symbol, was common to all nations of the earth from the earliest period."[1] Whereas Mackey was prone to the hyperbole, recorded history does reveal a long established use of the apron, or apron-like devices, as a symbol of investiture or membership in an organization whose very *raison d'etre* focused on the transfer of esoteric knowledge.

The apron worn by Freemasons, "resembles the girdle of the Israelite priest, the white apron of Mithras of Persia, the sash or zenner in India, the white robe of the Essenes, and similar symbols of the Ethiopians and Egyptians."[2] Whereas the apron was used in history symbolically. the color has not always been white. Dr. George Oliver, an English Freemason and prolific writer on Masonic subjects, wrote in *Signs and Symbols of Freemasonry* that throughout history symbolic aprons have not always been pure white, but rather they have been striped with various colors, decorated with gold, possessed fringes and/or tassels and often had linings of various colors, *i.e.* green in Ireland, naturally!

In addition to the color, the apron has not always been neatly rectangular. Operative masons had long aprons, aprons that often touched the knees and had round flaps that could be turned up and thus protect the workman's torso. In the transition from Operative to Speculative Freemasonry, the longer apron remained standard apparel for many years. A London engraver, William Hogart, made a rather famous picture entitled *Night* that depicts, in a somewhat unflattering manner, two English Freemasons making their way home after attending lodge one night. Clearly visible on the men are a Master's jewel, a Tyler's sword, candle-snuffers and Masonic aprons; aprons that extend below the knees. Along the same lines, Coil reports that two of George Washington's Masonic aprons, still preserved, also fall to knee level.

An extensive paper on the "Whys and Wherefores of the Masonic Apron," was presented by John Barr to the Masters and Past Masters' Lodge No. 130, Christ Church, New Zealand and is reported, in part, in Mackey's *Masonic Encyclopedia*. In his paper Barr makes relevant comments to this brief essay, but especially meaningful is his research into the first attempts at standardizing the size and color of Masonic aprons:

> The first attempt to create uniformity in the apron appears to have been in 1731...But all this was altered at the Union of Grand Lodges in 1813...[3]

Mr. Barr further states that there are two essential items to preserve the symbolic character of the apron — its

color and its material. He points out that the color of a Freemason's apron should be pure unspotted white. The key
word in the preceding sentence is, of course, "should."
Debaters will recall that the standard definition for the
word "should" is usually given as "ought to, but not necessarily will." White has been regarded as the color of innocence and purity and this thought is revealed in one of the
standard lectures given to newly made Freemasons when
being presented with their aprons.

> It is an emblem of innocence and the badge of a Mason. It is
> yours; yours to wear through an honorable life, and at your
> death to be placed upon the coffin which contains your
> earthly remains...Let its pure and spotless surface be to you
> an ever-present reminder of purity of life, of rectitude of
> conduct...

It is further pointed out that in the ancient Mysteries the
candidate was always clothed in white, the priests of Rome
were in white, the Druids preserved white for their last
degree or degree of perfection and in the early Christian
church a white garment was presented to the newly bap-
tized with the admonishment: "Receive the white and unde-
filed garment, and produce it unspotted before the tribunal
of our Lord Jesus Christ."

White, then, has a long historical basis for being adopted by Freemasons as the color of its apron. The material
was selected with equal thought and consideration.

The Freemason's apron has historically been made
of lambskin. In the first degree Masons are told that lambskin is to remind one of purity of life and, further, the lamb
in all ages has been the emblem of innocence. Again,
Freemasonry is not alone in the use of the lamb as a symbol. It should be recalled that the lamb is the church symbol
for Christ, whom John the Baptist called the Lamb of God.
The Jews have the Paschal Lamb, or the lamb offered as a
sacrifice at the Feast of Passover. In the Apocalypse it is
recorded that Saint John had a vision of Christ, in the form
of a lamb, wounded in the throat.

Historically, only the color and material was standard-
ized, but in the aforementioned Union of 1813 other items

were discussed. Entered Apprentice Masons, for example, were to have plain white lambskin aprons, 14 to 16 inches wide, 12 to 14 inches deep, square at the bottom, without adornment or ornamentation and with white strings. A Fellowcraft's apron had the identical size restrictions, but was allowed to have two sky-blue rosettes at the bottom. A Master Mason's apron had the same physical dimensions, but would also have sky-blue lining with the same colored edging, no more than 2 inches deep. An additional rosette on the flap was permitted as were silver tassels.

The 1813 decisions radically modified the Masonic apron and, in retrospect, created a dilemma. The shortening of the apron was, in and of itself, not exceptionally meaningful to Freemasonry. Although violence was done to the original functional design of the garment, the symbolic nature of the apron was retained. Yet, only the Entered Apprentice Mason's apron maintained its original symbolic design that focused on pureness and whiteness being emblematic of purity and innocence. The higher the degrees, the more ornamental, and less spotless and white, the apron became.

Although the 1813 decision applied only to the English lodges, there is evidence that other Freemasons also indulged in the practice of embellishing the apron.

> ...the silk or satin aprons, bespangled and painted and embroidered...have no connection with Ancient Craft Freemasonry. They are an innovation of our French Brethren...[4]

Mackey's aforestated comment illustrates that not all Freemasons were pleased with the practice of using the front of the apron to designate rank within the Masonic lodge, a lodge that prided itself on being classless and treating all as equals.

American Freemasonry has not escaped the trend that transformed the apron away from its original pure white design to a garment of increasingly elaborate design. On what was previously an unsullied white surface now can be found blazing suns, squares, compasses, levels, emblems of various lodge offices, wide and narrow edgings with linings of virtually every hue and color imaginable.

APRON PRESENTED TO GEORGE WASHINGTON BY LAFAYETTE

White Silk Apron hand-stitched by Madame LaFayette and presented to George Washington by the Marquis de LaFayette in 1784.

The apron embroidered for George Washington by the wife of General Lafayette has over three dozen Masonic symbols including four pillars, an all-seeing eye, square, compass, Bible, casket, sun, moon, and even two miniature statues. The only white on the apron provides background and relief — hardly a design conducive to focusing one's attention on the qualities of purity and innocence originally conceived by Masonic forefathers.

The contemporary Masonic apron has a long and noble heritage, tracing its roots, in concept, back to the ancient Mysteries and perhaps beyond. Although the shape has changed and even though the surface no longer bears a pure spotless appearance, the symbolic meaning remains constant.

Footnotes

[1] *Mackey's Revised Encyclopedia of Freemasonry*, p. 93.
[2] Henry Coil, *Masonic Encyclopedia*, p. 63.
[3] Mackey, *Op. cit.*, p. 95.
[4] *Ibid.*, p. 96.